쓰담쓰담

내신영문법

1

장재영

유명 어학원과 영어학원에서 강의하면서 강사, 부원장, 원장을 역임.
(전) 리딩스타어학원 디렉터
(전) 청담어학원 원장
(전) 아발론교육 원장
(현) 고려대학교 국제어학원 영어교육프로그램 EiE 원장
특목고 진로 컨설팅
저서『제대로 영작문』 시리즈

쓰담쓰담 내신영문법 1

지은이 장재영
펴낸이 정규도
펴낸곳 (주)다락원

초판 1쇄 발행 2017년 1월 5일
초판 3쇄 발행 2021년 8월 30일

편집 김민주, 김미경, 이동호
디자인 구수정
영문 감수 Michael A. Putlack
삽화 박하
조판 블랙 엔 화이트

다락원 경기도 파주시 문발로 211
내용문의 (02)736-2031 내선 503
구입문의 (02)736-2031 내선 250~252

Fax (02)732-2037
출판등록 1977년 9월 16일 제406-2008-000007호

값 11,000원

ISBN 978-89-277-0795-0 54740
978-89-277-0794-3 54740(set)

http://www.darakwon.co.kr

다락원 홈페이지를 방문하시면 상세한 출판정보와 함께
동영상강좌, MP3 자료 등 다양한 어학 정보를 얻으실 수 있습니다.

쓰담쓰담
내신영문법

1

이 책의 구성과 특징

핵심만 간추린 중요 문법 사항으로 문법의 기초를 다지고
서술형 위주로 엄선한 최신 기출 응용 문제로 내신 시험에 대비합니다.

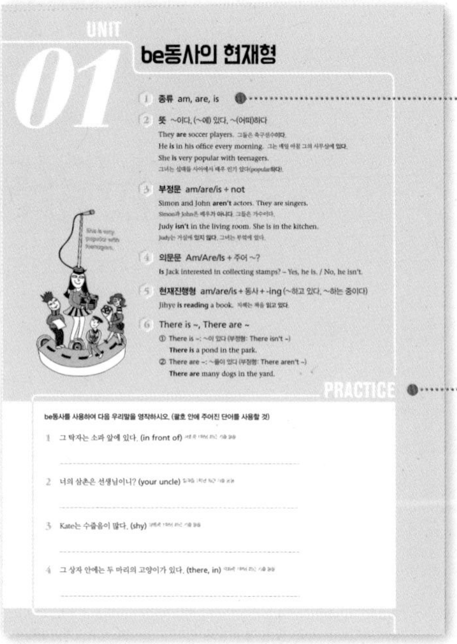
UNIT 01 be동사의 현재형

1 종류 am, are, is

2 뜻 ~이다, (~에) 있다, ~(어떠)하다
They **are** soccer players. 그들은 축구선수이다.
He **is** in his office every morning. 그는 매일 아침 그의 사무실에 있다.
She **is** very popular with teenagers.
그녀는 십대들 사이에서 매우 인기 있다(popular하다).

3 부정문 am/are/is + not
Simon and John **aren't** actors. They are singers.
Simon과 John은 배우가 아니다. 그들은 가수이다.
Judy **isn't** in the living room. She is in the kitchen.
Judy는 거실에 있지 않다. 그녀는 부엌에 있다.

4 의문문 Am/Are/Is + 주어 ~?
Is Jack interested in collecting stamps? – Yes, he is. / No, he isn't.

5 현재진행형 am/are/is + 동사 + -ing (~하고 있다, ~하는 중이다)
Jihye **is reading** a book. 지혜는 책을 읽고 있다.

6 There is ~, There are ~
① There is ~: ~이 있다 (부정형: There isn't ~)
There is a pond in the park.
② There are ~: ~들이 있다 (부정형: There aren't ~)
There are many dogs in the yard.

PRACTICE

be동사를 사용하여 다음 우리말을 영작하시오. (괄호 안에 주어진 단어를 사용할 것)

1 그 탁자는 소파 앞에 있다. (in front of)

2 너의 삼촌은 선생님이니? (your uncle)

3 Kate는 수줍음이 많다. (shy)

4 그 상자 안에는 두 마리의 고양이가 있다. (there, in)

핵심 문법 사항

중1 수준에서 반드시 알아야 할 중요 문법 사항들의 핵심만 간추려 정리했습니다.

PRACTICE

간단한 문장을 영작하면서 위에서 학습한 문법 사항을 점검해 봅니다.

연습문제는 모두 기출 응용 문제로 구성되어 있습니다.

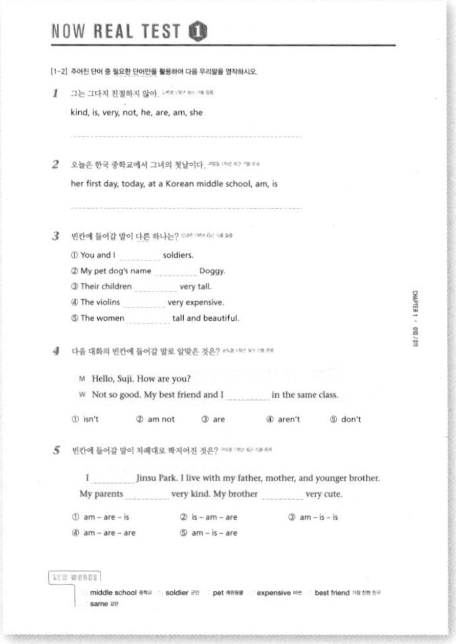
NOW REAL TEST 1

[1-2] 주어진 단어 중 필요한 단어만을 활용하여 다음 우리말을 영작하시오.

1 그는 그다지 친절하지 않아.
kind, is, very, not, he, are, am, she

2 오늘은 한국 중학교에서 그녀의 첫날이다.
her first day, today, at a Korean middle school, am, is

3 빈칸에 들어갈 말이 다른 하나는?
① You and I ________ soldiers.
② My pet dog's name ________ Doggy.
③ Their children ________ very tall.
④ The violins ________ very expensive.
⑤ The women ________ tall and beautiful.

4 다음 대화의 빈칸에 들어갈 말로 알맞은 것은?
M Hello, Suji. How are you?
W Not so good. My best friend and I ________ in the same class.
① isn't ② am not ③ are ④ aren't ⑤ don't

5 빈칸에 들어갈 말이 차례대로 짝지어진 것은?
I ________ Jinsu Park. I live with my father, mother, and younger brother.
My parents ________ very kind. My brother ________ very cute.
① am – are – is ② is – am – are ③ am – is – is
④ am – are – are ⑤ am – is – are

NEW WORDS
middle school 중학교 soldier 군인 pet 애완동물 expensive 비싼 best friend 가장 친한 친구
same 같은

CHAPTER 1 010 / 011

NOW REAL TEST 1
기출 응용 문제

7~10문항으로 구성된 최신 기출 응용 문제로 중학 내신 시험의 출제 경향을 파악할 수 있습니다.

서술형 문제 위주로 구성되어 있어, 학생들이 어려워하는 서술형 문제에 대비할 수 있습니다.

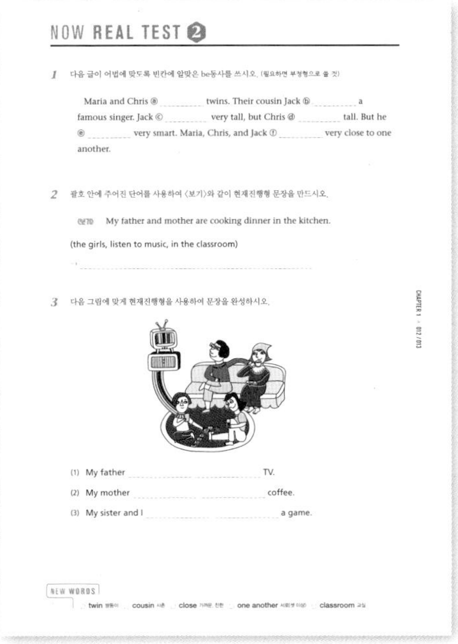

NOW REAL TEST 2

1 다음 글이 어법에 맞도록 빈칸에 알맞은 be동사를 쓰시오. (필요하면 부정형으로 쓸 것)

Maria and Chris ⓐ ________ twins. Their cousin Jack ⓑ ________ a famous singer. Jack ⓒ ________ very tall, but Chris ⓓ ________ tall. But he ⓔ ________ very smart. Maria, Chris, and Jack ⓕ ________ very close to one another.

2 괄호 안에 주어진 단어를 사용하여 〈보기〉와 같이 현재진행형 문장을 만드시오.

〈보기〉 My father and mother are cooking dinner in the kitchen.

(the girls, listen to music, in the classroom)

→ ______________________________

3 다음 그림에 맞게 현재진행형을 사용하여 문장을 완성하시오.

(1) My father ________ ________ TV.
(2) My mother ________ ________ coffee.
(3) My sister and I ________ ________ a game.

CHAPTER 1 · 012 / 013

NEW WORDS
twin 쌍둥이 cousin 사촌 close 가까운, 친한 one another 서로(셋 이상) classroom 교실

NOW REAL TEST 2

실전 예상 문제

3~6문항으로 구성된 실전 예상 문제로 내신 시험에 본격적으로 대비합니다.

서술형 문제 위주로 구성되어 있어, 학생들이 어려워하는 서술형 문제에 대비할 수 있습니다.

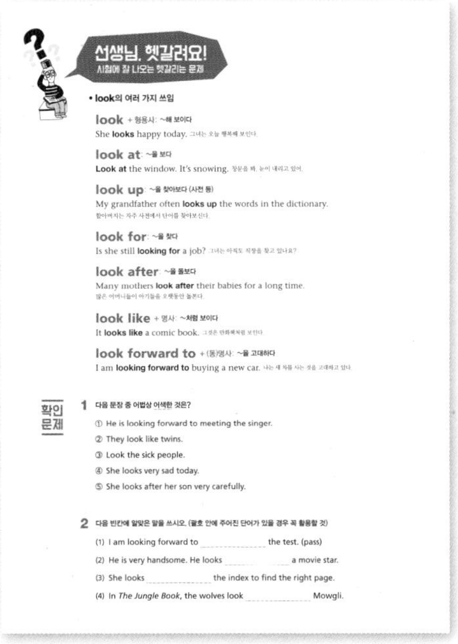

선생님, 헷갈려요!
시험에 잘 나오는 헷갈리는 문제

• look의 여러 가지 쓰임

look + 형용사: ~해 보이다
She **looks** happy today. 그녀는 오늘 행복해 보인다.

look at: ~을 보다
Look at the window. It's snowing. 창문을 봐. 눈이 내리고 있어.

look up: ~을 찾아보다 (사전 등)
My grandfather often **looks up** the words in the dictionary.
할아버지는 자주 사전에서 단어를 찾아보신다.

look for: ~을 찾다
Is she still **looking for** a job? 그녀는 아직도 직장을 찾고 있나요?

look after: ~을 돌보다
Many mothers **look after** their babies for a long time.
많은 어머니들이 아기들을 오랫동안 돌본다.

look like + 명사: ~처럼 보이다
It **looks like** a comic book. 그것은 만화책처럼 보인다.

look forward to + (동)명사: ~을 고대하다
I am **looking forward to** buying a new car. 나는 새 차를 사는 것을 고대하고 있다.

확인문제

1 다음 문장 중 어법상 어색한 것은?
① He is looking forward to meeting the singer.
② They look like twins.
③ Look the sick people.
④ She looks very sad today.
⑤ She looks after her son very carefully.

2 다음 빈칸에 알맞은 말을 쓰시오. (괄호 안에 주어진 단어가 있을 경우 꼭 활용할 것)
(1) I am looking forward to ________ the test. (pass)
(2) He is very handsome. He looks ________ a movie star.
(3) She looks ________ the index to find the right page.
(4) In *The Jungle Book*, the wolves look ________ Mowgli.

선생님, 헷갈려요!

시험에 잘 나오는 헷갈리는 문제

학생들이 잘 모르거나 헷갈려 하는 문법 사항, 구동사, 관용 표현 등을 짚고 넘어가는 코너입니다.

특히 시험에 잘 나오는 항목으로 엄선하여 내신 시험에 효과적으로 대비합니다.

차례

Chapter 1

동사의 현재형

UNIT 01 be동사의 현재형

UNIT 02 일반동사의 현재형

UNIT 01

be동사의 현재형

1 종류 am, are, is

2 뜻 ~이다, (~에) 있다, ~(어떠)하다

They **are** soccer players. 그들은 축구선수**이다**.

He **is** in his office every morning. 그는 매일 아침 그의 사무실에 **있다**.

She **is** very popular with teenagers.
그녀는 십대들 사이에서 매우 인기 있다(popular**하다**).

3 부정문 am/are/is + not

Simon and John **aren't** actors. They are singers.
Simon과 John은 배우**가 아니다**. 그들은 가수이다.

Judy **isn't** in the living room. She is in the kitchen.
Judy는 거실에 **있지 않다**. 그녀는 부엌에 있다.

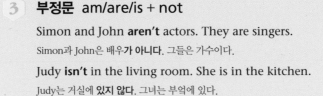

4 의문문 Am/Are/Is + 주어 ~?

Is Jack interested in collecting stamps? – Yes, he is. / No, he isn't.

5 현재진행형 am/are/is + 동사 + -ing (~하고 있다, ~하는 중이다)

Jihye **is reading** a book. 지혜는 책을 **읽고 있다**.

6 There is ~, There are ~

① There is ~: ~이 있다 (부정형: There isn't ~)
There is a pond in the park.

② There are ~: ~들이 있다 (부정형: There aren't ~)
There are many dogs in the yard.

PRACTICE

be동사를 사용하여 다음 우리말을 영작하시오. (괄호 안에 주어진 단어를 사용할 것)

1 그 탁자는 소파 앞에 있다. (in front of) 서초중 1학년 최근 기출 응용

2 너의 삼촌은 선생님이니? (your uncle) 임곡중 1학년 최근 기출 응용

3 Kate는 수줍음이 많다. (shy) 양동중 1학년 최근 기출 응용

4 그 상자 안에는 두 마리의 고양이가 있다. (there, in) 덕화중 1학년 최근 기출 응용

NOW REAL TEST 1

[1-2] 주어진 단어 중 필요한 단어만을 활용하여 다음 우리말을 영작하시오.

1 그는 그다지 친절하지 않아. 고명중 1학년 최근 기출 응용

kind, is, very, not, he, are, am, she

____

2 오늘은 한국 중학교에서 그녀의 첫날이다. 대림중 1학년 최근 기출 응용

her first day, today, at a Korean middle school, am, is

____

3 빈칸에 들어갈 말이 다른 하나는? 안양중 1학년 최근 기출 응용

① You and I ________ soldiers.

② My pet dog's name ________ Doggy.

③ Their children ________ very tall.

④ The violins ________ very expensive.

⑤ The women ________ tall and beautiful.

4 다음 대화의 빈칸에 들어갈 말로 알맞은 것은? 동도중 1학년 최근 기출 응용

M Hello, Suji. How are you?
W Not so good. My best friend and I ________ in the same class.

① isn't ② am not ③ are ④ aren't ⑤ don't

5 빈칸에 들어갈 말이 차례대로 짝지어진 것은? 구미중 1학년 최근 기출 응용

I ________ Jinsu Park. I live with my father, mother, and younger brother. My parents ________ very kind. My brother ________ very cute.

① am – are – is ② is – am – are ③ am – is – is
④ am – are – are ⑤ am – is – are

NEW WORDS

□ **middle school** 중학교 □ **soldier** 군인 □ **pet** 애완동물 □ **expensive** 비싼 □ **best friend** 가장 친한 친구
□ **same** 같은

6 다음 글에서 틀린 곳을 찾아 바르게 고쳐서 전체 내용을 다시 쓰시오. 신곡중 1학년 최근 기출 응용

My friend Jongin and I am good friends. We are in the same class. Our teachers is very kind.

→ ______

______

7 다음 대화의 빈칸에 공통으로 들어갈 알맞은 말을 쓰시오. 초지중 1학년 최근 기출 응용

A What ______ that in her hand?

B It ______ her movie ticket collection.

8 괄호 안의 표현을 이용하여 〈보기〉와 같이 대화를 완성하시오. (대소문자와 문장부호에 유의할 것) 서라벌중 1학년 최근 기출 응용

〈보기〉 Larry is in his office.

A Is Larry playing baseball? (play baseball)

B No, he isn't. He is sending an email. (send an email)

Sera is in her room.

A ⓐ ______ (ride a bike)

B No, she isn't. ⓑ ______ (do her homework)

9 다음 메모는 글쓴이의 강아지에 대한 정보를 나타낸 것이다. 메모의 내용과 일치하도록 빈칸에 알맞은 문장을 쓰시오. 광덕중 1학년 최근 기출 응용

〈MEMO〉
- 이름: Kelly
- 나이: 2살
- 특징: 작고 하얀색임. 곱슬곱슬한 털을 가짐.

→ This is my dog Kelly. It is 2 years old. ______ It has curly hair.

NEW WORDS

□ movie ticket 영화 표 □ collection 모음집, 수집품 □ office 사무실 □ send 보내다 □ ride a bike 자전거를 타다 □ curly 곱슬곱슬한

NOW REAL TEST 2

1 다음 글이 어법에 맞도록 빈칸에 알맞은 be동사를 쓰시오. (필요하면 부정형으로 쓸 것)

Maria and Chris ⓐ __________ twins. Their cousin Jack ⓑ __________ a famous singer. Jack ⓒ __________ very tall, but Chris ⓓ __________ tall. But he ⓔ __________ very smart. Maria, Chris, and Jack ⓕ __________ very close to one another.

2 괄호 안에 주어진 단어를 사용하여 〈보기〉와 같이 현재진행형 문장을 만드시오.

〈보기〉 My father and mother are cooking dinner in the kitchen.

(the girls, listen to music, in the classroom)

→ ______________________________

3 다음 그림에 맞게 현재진행형을 사용하여 문장을 완성하시오.

(1) My father __________ __________ TV.

(2) My mother __________ __________ coffee.

(3) My sister and I __________ __________ a game.

NEW WORDS

□ twin 쌍둥이 □ cousin 사촌 □ close 가까운, 친한 □ one another 서로(셋 이상) □ classroom 교실

4 다음은 래원이의 오답노트이다. 각 항목에서 틀린 부분을 찾아 바르게 고쳐 쓰시오.

날짜	3월 3일
문제 출처	교과서 1단원 p.24
난이도	★★ ☆ ☆ ☆
틀린 문장	(1) Is peter and Harry your friends? (2) Mr. James are a good cook. (3) My aunt is a music teacher. 　　They are very nice to me.

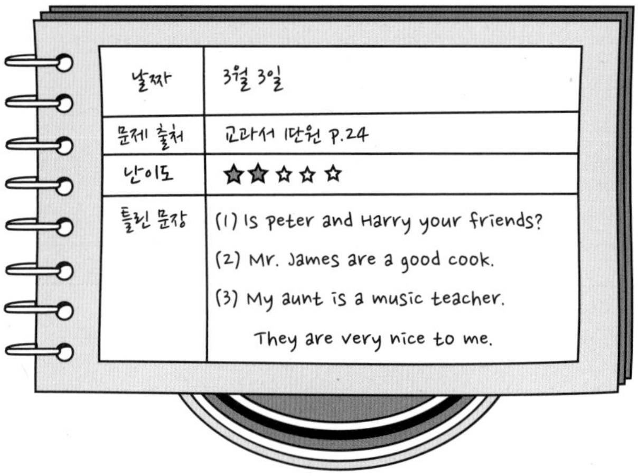

(1) _____ → _____

(2) _____ → _____

(3) _____ → _____

5 다음 우리말을 괄호 안에 주어진 단어와 현재진행형을 사용하여 영작하시오.

(1) Jimmy는 무엇을 하고 있는 중이니? (do)

→ _____

(2) 그녀는 정원에서 식물에게 물을 주고 있어. (water the plants)

→ _____

6 다음 글에서 어법상 틀린 문장을 3개 찾아서 밑줄을 긋고, 올바른 문장으로 고쳐 쓰시오.

There is a school concert today. Everything is ready, and many guests is coming. There is many good dancers in our school. Jeongmin and Minjeong is good at dancing. They will dance to the music.

→ _____

NEW WORDS

☐ **cook** 요리사 ☐ **aunt** 이모, 고모, (외)숙모 ☐ **water** 물을 주다 ☐ **plant** 식물 ☐ **guest** 손님
☐ **be good at** ~을 잘하다

UNIT 02

일반동사의 현재형

1 쓰임 현재의 반복적 행동이나 습관, 또는 일반적 사실을 나타낼 때 사용한다.

He **goes** to school by bus. 그는 버스를 타고 학교에 **간다**.

cf. 현재진행형과의 비교: 현재진행형은 현재 하고 있는 행동을 표현할 때 사용한다.

You play the guitar. 너는 기타를 친다. (기타를 칠 줄 알고 치는 사람이다.)

You are playing the guitar now. 너는 지금 기타를 치고 있다. (기타 치는 행위 표현)

2 3인칭 단수가 주어일 때 동사 뒤에 -s나 -es를 붙인다.

① 일반적 경우: -s를 붙인다.

He **runs** very fast.

② ch, sh, o, s, x, z로 끝나는 경우: -es를 붙인다.

He **washes** his car every day.

③ '자음 + y'로 끝나는 경우: y를 i로 바꾸고 -es를 붙인다.

The baby **cries** every morning.

He washes his car every day.

3 부정문 don't + 동사원형 / doesn't + 동사원형

*doesn't는 주어가 3인칭 단수일 때 사용한다.

They **don't want** to stay here. 그들은 여기 머물고 **싶어 하지 않는다**.

Michael **doesn't like** horror movies. Michael은 공포 영화를 **좋아하지 않는다**.

4 의문문 Do + 주어 + 동사원형 ~? / Does + 주어 + 동사원형 ~?

*Does는 주어가 3인칭 단수일 때 사용한다.

Do they **like** pizza? – Yes, they do. / No, they don't.

Does Jane **play** the piano every day?

– Yes, she does. / No, she doesn't.

PRACTICE

다음 우리말을 영작하시오. (괄호 안에 주어진 단어를 사용할 것)

1 그는 늦게 자러 간다. (late) 신덕중 1학년 최신 기출 응용

2 나는 자전거를 타고 학교에 가지 않는다. (go, by bike) 광덕중 1학년 최신 기출 응용

3 그녀는 매일 아침 조깅을 하러 가니? (go jogging) 방탄중 1학년 최신 기출 응용

4 어떤 동물들은 그들의 꼬리를 사용하지 않는다. (some animals, use, their tails) 송호중 1학년 최신 기출 응용

NOW REAL TEST 1

1 다음 괄호 안에서 어법에 맞는 것을 골라 ○표 하시오. 동신중 1학년 최근 기출 응용

(1) He (have / has) a lot of homework.

(2) Jin (go / goes) to bed early every night.

(3) Sam (don't / doesn't) like pizza.

2 다음 중 어법에 맞지 않는 것은? 발곡중 1학년 최근 기출 응용

① Jaesoek comes home from school around 4 o'clock.
② He always throws his socks on the sofa.
③ They doesn't need us.
④ His dad takes care of the dogs.
⑤ Do you need any help?

3 괄호 안의 단어를 순서대로 맞게 배열했을 때 세 번째로 오는 단어를 쓰시오. 공주북중 1학년 최근 기출 응용

We (on / to / go / don't / school) Sundays.

→ ____________

4 다음 문장의 빈칸에 들어갈 말로 적절하지 않은 것은? 계성중 1학년 최근 기출 응용

________ gets up very late in the morning.

① He ② Jinsu and Najin ③ Sam's brother
④ Your sister ⑤ My friend Jack

5 다음 문장 중 어법상 어색한 것은? 광희중 1학년 최근 기출 응용

① I don't like comic books.
② Bora watches TV every evening.
③ My parents washes their cars every Sunday.
④ Some people don't drink coffee in the evening.
⑤ My computer works very well.

NEW WORDS

□ **homework** 숙제 □ **go to bed** 잠자리에 들다 □ **around** ~경에 □ **o'clock** ~시 □ **take care of** ~을 돌보다
□ **comic book** 만화책 □ **work** 작동하다

6 다음 문장 중 어법상 올바른 것은? 봉명여중 1학년 최근 기출 응용

① My brother Minjun go to elementary school.

② My uncle makes toy cars.

③ It don't work well.

④ They doesn't sell hamburgers.

⑤ He doesn't stops studying.

7 다음 우리말에 맞게 빈칸에 알맞은 말을 쓰시오. 강현중 1학년 최근 기출 응용

해영은 개를 한 마리 가지고 있지만 도경이는 개를 가지고 있지 않다.

→ Haeyeong ________ a dog, but Dogyeong ________ a dog.

8 괄호 안의 단어 중 알맞은 것에 ○표 하시오. 명덕여중 1학년 최근 기출 응용

(1) Hijin doesn't (like / likes) fishing, but her dad really (like / likes) it.

(2) Does your mom (cook / cooks) very well?

9 빈칸에 들어갈 말이 나머지와 다른 하나는? 개림중 1학년 최근 기출 응용

① ________ they like soccer?

② ________ Yujin play computer games every day?

③ ________ Sue and John swim very well?

④ ________ Mr. Kim and Mrs. Yi live in Seoul?

⑤ ________ the students do their homework every day?

10 다음 우리말에 맞게 빈칸에 알맞은 말을 쓰시오. 동백중 1학년 최근 기출 응용

A 그들은 캐나다에 사니?
B 아니, 그렇지 않아. 그들은 호주에 살아.

A ________ they ________ in Canada?

B No, ________ ________. They live in Australia.

NEW WORDS

□ elementary school 초등학교 □ fishing 낚시 □ cook 요리하다 □ Australia 호주

NOW REAL TEST 2

1 다음 표는 두 사람의 취미 생활을 나타낸 것이다. 표에 관한 대화의 빈칸에 알맞은 대답을 쓰시오.

	Read Books	Play the Piano	Play the Guitar
Jack	○	×	○
Jennifer	○	○	×

*Jack은 남자, Jennifer는 여자

(1) A Does Jack read books?

B ______________, ______________ ______________.

(2) A Does Jennifer play the guitar?

B ______________, ______________ ______________.

2 다음 문장을 괄호 안의 지시대로 바꾸어 쓰시오.

(1) Brian goes to the movies once a month. (부정문으로)

→ ______________________________

(2) Sally cleans her room every day. (의문문으로)

→ ______________________________

3 다음 각 문장의 주어를 'I'가 아닌 'He'로 바꾸어 문장 전체를 다시 쓰시오.

I like music. I play the piano well. I often go to classical music concerts with my friends.

→ ______________________________

____

NEW WORDS

- □ go to the movies 영화를 보러 가다 □ once 한 번 □ often 종종, 자주 □ classical 클래식의
- □ concert 연주회, 콘서트

4 다음 글을 읽고, 물음에 답하시오.

My name is Olivia. I have two little sisters, Judy and Sue. I teach English to Judy. I play ball with Sue.

(1) Does Olivia have two sisters?

→ ______ ______________________

(2) Does Olivia teach math to Judy?

→ ______________________

5 다음은 수지(Suji)가 해야 할 일을 나타낸 표이다. 수지가 금요일에 하는 것과 하지 않는 것을 잘 구별하여 빈칸에 알맞은 말을 쓰시오. (현재형만 사용할 것)

*사용해야 할 동사: clean, wash, feed, water

Wed.	○	○	×	○	×
Thurs.	○	○	○	○	×
Fri.	○	○	×	○	○

On Friday, Suji ________ the living room, ________ the dishes, ________ the dog, and ________ the flowers. But she ________ ________ the bathroom on that day.

NEW WORDS

□ teach 가르치다 □ play ball 공놀이를 하다 □ feed 먹이를 주다

선생님, 헷갈려요!
시험에 잘 나오는 헷갈리는 문제

- **look의 여러 가지 쓰임**

look + 형용사: ~해 보이다

She **looks** happy today. 그녀는 오늘 행복해 보인다.

look at: ~을 보다

Look at the window. It's snowing. 창문을 봐. 눈이 내리고 있어.

look up: ~을 찾아보다 (사전 등)

My grandfather often **looks up** the words in the dictionary.
할아버지는 자주 사전에서 단어를 찾아보신다.

look for: ~을 찾다

Is she still **looking for** a job? 그녀는 아직도 직장을 찾고 있나요?

look after: ~을 돌보다

Many mothers **look after** their babies for a long time.
많은 어머니들이 아기들을 오랫동안 돌본다.

look like + 명사: ~처럼 보이다

It **looks like** a comic book. 그것은 만화책처럼 보인다.

look forward to + (동)명사: ~을 고대하다

I am **looking forward to** buying a new car. 나는 새 차를 사는 것을 고대하고 있다.

확인문제

1 다음 문장 중 어법상 어색한 것은?

① He is looking forward to meeting the singer.

② They look like twins.

③ Look the sick people.

④ She looks very sad today.

⑤ She looks after her son very carefully.

2 다음 빈칸에 알맞은 말을 쓰시오. (괄호 안에 주어진 단어가 있을 경우 꼭 활용할 것)

(1) I am looking forward to ______________ the test. (pass)

(2) He is very handsome. He looks ______________ a movie star.

(3) She looks ______________ the index to find the right page.

(4) In *The Jungle Book*, the wolves look ______________ Mowgli.

Chapter 2

동사의 과거형

UNIT 03

be동사의 과거형

1 **종류** was, were

2 **뜻** ~였다, (~에) 있었다, ~(어떠)했다

My father **was** a volleyball player. 아버지는 배구선수**였다**.

Your keys **were** on the sofa. 너의 열쇠는 소파 위에 **있었다**.

My grandmother **was** creative. 할머니는 창의적**이셨다**(creative**했었다**).

3 **부정문** was/were + not

He **wasn't** a soldier at that time. 그는 그 당시에 군인**이 아니었다**.

John and Sue **weren't** in Seoul in 2010.
John과 Sue는 2010년에 서울에 **있지 않았다**.

He **wasn't** tired after school yesterday. 그는 어제 방과 후에 피곤**하지 않았다**.

4 **의문문** Was/Were + 주어 ~?

Was Tom responsible for the results? Tom이 그 결과에 책임이 있었니?
– Yes, he was. / No, he wasn't.

5 **과거진행형** was/were + 동사 + -ing (~하고 있었다, ~하는 중이었다)

The rabbits **were eating** some carrots. 그 토끼들은 약간의 당근을 **먹고 있었다**.

6 There was ~, There were ~

① There was ~: ~이 있었다 (부정형: There wasn't ~)
There was a big tree in front of your house.

② There were ~: ~들이 있었다 (부정형: There weren't ~)
There were many doves in the park.

My father was a volleyball player.

PRACTICE

be동사의 과거형을 사용하여 다음 우리말을 영작하시오. (괄호 안에 주어진 단어를 사용할 것)

1 작년에 나는 매우 아팠다. (ill, I, very, last) 거성중 1학년 최근 기출 응용

____

2 공원에 많은 사람들이 있었다. (there, in the park, many) 고대부속중 1학년 최근 기출 응용

____

3 너 어제 YG 콘서트에 있었니? (at the YG concert) 광희중 1학년 최근 기출 응용

____

4 그 문제는 매우 어렵지는 않았다. (the question, difficult) 경성중 1학년 최근 기출 응용

____

NOW REAL TEST 1

[1-2] 주어진 단어를 사용하여 우리말을 영작하시오.

1 김연아는 빙판에서 스케이트를 타고 있었다. 구로중 1학년 최근 기출 응용

Kim Yuna, on the ice, skate

____

2 나는 어젯밤에 테니스를 치고 있었다. 관양중 1학년 최근 기출 응용

play tennis, last

____

3 다음 중 어법상 옳지 않은 것은? 공릉중 1학년 최근 기출 응용

① He and I was in the park last weekend.

② We were playing games at that time.

③ Were you in the living room at 10?

④ How was she yesterday?

⑤ There was a cute cat in the yard yesterday.

4 다음 중 빈칸에 들어갈 말이 나머지와 다른 하나는? 계산중 1학년 최근 기출 응용

① There ________ many books on the desk yesterday.

② There ________ a park by the building when I was young.

③ There ________ two girls on the bench 30 minutes ago.

④ There ________ over ten people in the gym last night.

⑤ There ________ some monkeys at the zoo this morning.

5 다음 문장을 읽고, 질문에 대한 답을 영어로 쓰시오. 상경중 1학년 최근 기출 응용

Mr. Kim was in the gym for playing basketball yesterday.

Q What was Mr. Kim doing in the gym yesterday?

→ ______________________________

NEW WORDS

☐ skate 스케이트를 타다 ☐ weekend 주말 ☐ at that time 그때, 당시에 ☐ living room 거실 ☐ yard 마당
☐ over ~이 넘는 ☐ gym 체육관, 헬스클럽

6 주어진 단어를 활용하여 우리말을 조건에 맞게 영작하시오. 반포중 1학년 최근 기출 응용

me, woman, taste, next to

〈조건〉 총 8단어가 되도록 하되 필요하면 형태를 변형시킬 것

한 여자가 내 옆에서 김치(kimchi)를 맛보고 있었다.

→ ______________________________

7 다음 문장 중 어법상 올바른 것은? 거제여중 1학년 최근 기출 응용

① I were hungry because I did lots of work.

② There was money, bread, and some cookies on the kitchen table.

③ There were some milk in the glass.

④ Were there some workers in that factory?

⑤ Mr. Davis were playing soccer with his friends yesterday.

8 다음 그림을 보고, 질문에 과거진행형으로 답하시오. 연화중 1학년 최근 기출 응용

Q What was Minsu doing yesterday?

A ______________________________

NEW WORDS

□ taste 맛보다 □ next to ~ 옆에서 □ lots of 많은 □ worker 일꾼 □ factory 공장

9 다음 질문에 대한 대답으로 가장 적절한 것은? 신남중 1학년 최근 기출 응용

Q Wasn't Sam in Seoul last year?

① No, he didn't.
② Yes, he did.
③ No, he wasn't.
④ Yes, he didn't.
⑤ No, he was in Seoul.

10 다음 우리말을 영어로 가장 바르게 옮긴 것은?

그가 햄버거를 먹고 있었나요?

① Did he eat a hamburger?
② Was he ate a hamburger?
③ Does he ate a hamburger?
④ Was he eat a hamburger?
⑤ Was he eating a hamburger?

NOW REAL TEST 2

1 다음 표는 엄마가 지홍(Jihong)이에게 하고 있으라고 지시한 일이다. 지홍이가 하고 있었던 일 두 가지와 하고 있지 않았던 일 두 가지를 과거진행형으로 쓰시오.

엄마의 지시	실행 여부
"Do your homework."	○
"Clean your room."	×
"Wash the dishes."	×
"Take care of your younger brother."	○

(1) 하고 있었던 일

Jihong ______________________________.

Jihong ______________________________.

(2) 하고 있지 않았던 일

Jihong ______________________________.

Jihong ______________________________.

2 주어진 단어를 알맞게 변형하여 다음 우리말을 영작하시오.

내가 판소리 공연을 보고 있었을 때 엄마는 떡을 만들고 계셨다.

(*pansori* performance, make, rice cakes, when, watch, my mom)

→ ______________________________

NEW WORDS

□ performance 공연 □ rice cake 떡

3 다음 대화를 읽고, 밑줄 친 (가)와 (나)를 영작하시오.

M Hi, Lily. Where were you last night?
W (가) 나는 도서관에 있었어.
M What were you doing there?
W (나) 나는 몇 권의 과학 책을 읽고 있었어.

(가) ______

(나) ______

4 다음 질문과 대답을 영작하시오.

Q 그 동물원에는 많은 사자들이 있었니?
A 응, 거기에는 네 마리의 사자들이 있었어.

Q ______

A ______

NEW WORDS

□ library 도서관 □ science 과학

UNIT 04

일반동사의 과거형

1 형태

① 대부분의 동사: 동사 + -ed (예: played, jumped)

② -e로 끝나는 동사: + -d (예: liked, lived)

③ '자음 + y'로 끝나는 동사: y를 i로 바꾸고 + -ed (예: carried, studied)

④ '단모음 + 단자음'으로 끝나는 동사:
자음 하나 더 쓰고 + -ed (예: stopped, jogged)

⑤ 불규칙 동사: 암기 필요 (예: see – saw, buy – bought)

2 쓰임

① 과거의 특정한 때의 일을 나타낼 때

He **lived** in Japan last year. 그는 작년에 일본에서 **살았다.**

② 역사적 사실을 나타낼 때

King Sejong **invented** Hangeul. 세종대왕은 한글을 **발명했다.**

King Sejong invented Hangeul.

3 부정문 didn't + 동사원형

Song Junggi **didn't buy** a new car. 송중기는 새 차를 **사지 않았다.**

4 의문문 Did + 주어 + 동사원형 ~?

Did you **send** an email to Han Hyoju? 너 한효주에게 이메일 **보냈니?**
– Yes, I did. / No, I didn't.

PRACTICE

다음 우리말을 영작하시오. (괄호 안에 주어진 단어를 사용할 것)

1 Molly는 집 여기저기를 뛰어다녔다. (around the house) 개림중 1학년 최신 기출 응용

____

2 그는 오늘 일찍 일어나지 않았다. (early) 개운중 1학년 최신 기출 응용

____

3 나의 부모님은 어제 커피를 많이 드셨다. (drink, a lot of) 신목중 1학년 최신 기출 응용

____

4 호동(Hodong)이는 저녁으로 고기를 먹지 않았다. (meat, for dinner) 목동중 1학년 최신 기출 응용

____

NOW REAL TEST 1

1 괄호 안에서 어법에 맞는 것을 고르시오. 원촌중 1학년 최근 기출 응용

(1) He (has / had) dinner with her yesterday.

(2) Did she (go / went) to school yesterday?

(3) Steve (didn't buy / doesn't bought) the car.

2 다음 중 빈칸에 들어갈 말이 어법상 옳은 것은? 난우중 1학년 최근 기출 응용

What did he ________ last weekend?

① does ② buys ③ do
④ sent ⑤ made

3 괄호 안에 주어진 단어를 활용하여 빈칸에 알맞은 말을 시제에 맞게 쓰시오. 가락중 1학년 최근 기출 응용

I usually get up early in the morning. But yesterday I ________ ________ ________ early. So I was late. (get up)

4 다음 우리말을 영작하시오. 신정중 1학년 최근 기출 응용

나의 수학 선생님은 오늘 학교에 오시지 않으셨다.

→ ________________________________

5 다음 중 동사의 과거형이 잘못 짝지어진 것은? 공릉중 1학년 최신 기출 응용

① are – were ② eat – ate ③ take – took
④ sleep – sleeped ⑤ make – made

NEW WORDS

□ buy 사다 □ usually 주로, 보통

6 다음 지나간 일정표를 보고, 빈칸에 알맞은 표현을 과거형으로 쓰시오. 관양중 1학년 최근 기출 응용

Monday	Play Tennis
Wednesday	See a Movie
Friday	Eat Out

(1) I ______________________ last Monday.

(2) I ______________________ last Wednesday.

(3) I ______________________ last Friday.

7 다음 체크리스트를 보고 어제 한 일과 하지 않았던 일을 각각 쓰시오. 원일중 1학년 최근 기출 응용

watch TV (○) eat breakfast (×) water the plants (○) meet my friends (×)

(1) 어제 한 일

I ______________________ yesterday.

I ______________________ yesterday.

(2) 어제 하지 않았던 일

I ______________________ yesterday.

I ______________________ yesterday.

8 다음 대화의 빈칸 ⓐ~ⓓ에 알맞은 말을 쓰시오. 배재중 1학년 최근 기출 응용

A ⓐ __________ Jeongsu wake up at 7 o'clock this morning?

B No, ⓑ ______________.

A ⓒ __________ he bring his English book?

B Yes, ⓓ ______________.

NEW WORDS

□ eat out 외식하다 □ wake up 잠에서 깨다 □ bring 가지고 오다

금명중 1학년 최근 기출 응용

9 다음 그림을 보고, 소년이 어젯밤에 한 일과 하지 않은 일을 주어진 동사를 활용하여 빈칸에 쓰시오.

○	×

(1) He ______________ pizza last night. (eat)

(2) He ______________ computer games last night. (play)

10 주어진 단어를 활용해서 빈칸에 알맞은 말을 과거형으로 쓰시오. 개림중 1학년 최근 기출 응용

(1) She __________ outside for a walk. (go)

(2) They __________ married. (get)

(3) Jeongin __________ into a new apartment. (move)

NEW WORDS

□ go for a walk 산책하러 가다 □ outside 밖으로 □ get married 결혼하다 □ apartment 아파트

NOW REAL TEST 2

1 다음 글에서 어법상 틀린 동사 4개를 찾아 시제에 맞게 고쳐 쓰시오.

I visit my uncle last week. There were two big dogs. I feed them instead of my uncle. There was also a cute kitten. It jump on me. My uncle called me to dinner. I have a delicious dinner with him. I was very happy there.

______ → ______ ______ → ______

______ → ______ ______ → ______

2 다음 문장을 과거형으로 고쳐 쓰시오.

(1) They want to go to Jeju.

→ ______

(2) My father buys groceries at the supermarket.

→ ______

(3) She cuts the cake into two pieces.

→ ______

3 다음은 수진이의 오답노트이다. 수진이가 고친 내용 중 틀린 것을 2개 골라 그 문장을 바르게 쓰시오.

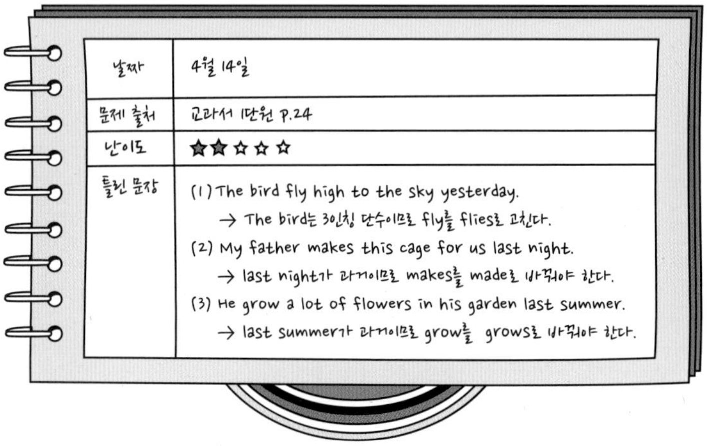

날짜	4월 14일
문제 출처	교과서 1단원 p.24
난이도	★★☆☆☆
틀린 문장	(1) The bird fly high to the sky yesterday. → The bird는 3인칭 단수이므로 fly를 flies로 고친다. (2) My father makes this cage for us last night. → last night가 과거이므로 makes를 made로 바꿔야 한다. (3) He grow a lot of flowers in his garden last summer. → last summer가 과거이므로 grow를 grows로 바꿔야 한다.

→ ______

______

NEW WORDS

□ visit 방문하다 □ instead of ~ 대신에 □ kitten 새끼 고양이 □ groceries 식료품 □ cut A into B A를 B로 자르다
□ piece 조각 □ cage 새장, 우리 □ grow 기르다

4 다음 문장을 괄호 안의 지시대로 바꾸어 쓰시오.

(1) He sent an email to her last night. (의문문으로)

→ ______________________________

(2) Paul and Emma fixed the broken machine. (부정문으로)

→ ______________________________

5 괄호 안에 주어진 단어를 사용하여 다음 우리말 대화를 영작하시오.

A 한국전쟁(the Korean War)이 1951년에 일어났니? (break out)

B 아니, 그렇지 않아. 그건 1950년에 일어났어.

A ______________________________

B ______________________________

NEW WORDS

□ fix 고치다 □ broken 고장 난 □ machine 기계 □ the Korean War 한국전쟁(6.25) □ break out 발발하다

선생님, 헷갈려요!

시험에 잘 나오는 헷갈리는 문제

시험에 잘 나오는 가장 기본적인 불규칙 동사 변화 55

	뜻	현재	과거	과거분사
1	되다	become	became	become
2	시작하다	begin	began	begun
3	물다	bite	bit	bitten
4	(바람이) 불다	blow	blew	blown
5	깨뜨리다	break	broke	broken
6	가지고 오다	bring	brought	brought
7	짓다	build	built	built
8	사다	buy	bought	bought
9	잡다	catch	caught	caught
10	선택하다	choose	chose	chosen
11	파다	dig	dug	dug
12	하다	do	did	done
13	그리다	draw	drew	drawn
14	마시다	drink	drank	drunk
15	운전하다	drive	drove	driven
16	먹다	eat	ate	eaten
17	떨어지다	fall	fell	fallen
18	먹이를 주다	feed	fed	fed
19	느끼다	feel	felt	felt
20	찾다	find	found	found
21	날다	fly	flew	flown
22	잊다	forget	forgot	forgot(ten)
23	얻다	get	got	got(ten)
24	주다	give	gave	given
25	자라다	grow	grew	grown
26	가지다	have	had	had
27	듣다	hear	heard	heard
28	숨기다, 숨다	hide	hid	hidden
29	지키다	keep	kept	kept
30	알다	know	knew	known
31	떠나다, 남기다	leave	left	left
32	빌려주다	lend	lent	lent
33	잃어버리다	lose	lost	lost
34	만들다	make	made	made
35	만나다	meet	met	met
36	올라타다	ride	rode	ridden
37	달리다	run	ran	run
38	말하다	say	said	said
39	팔다	sell	sold	sold
40	보내다	send	sent	sent
41	노래하다	sing	sang	sung
42	앉다	sit	sat	sat
43	자다	sleep	slept	slept
44	말하다	speak	spoke	spoken
45	쓰다(돈,시간)	spend	spent	spent
46	서다	stand	stood	stood
47	훔치다	steal	stole	stolen
48	수영하다	swim	swam	swum
49	가지고 가다	take	took	taken
50	가르치다	teach	taught	taught
51	말하다	tell	told	told
52	생각하다	think	thought	thought
53	던지다	throw	threw	thrown
54	이기다	win	won	won
55	글 쓰다	write	wrote	written

Chapter 3

조동사

UNIT 05 will, be going to, can, be able to

UNIT 06 must, should, have to, may

UNIT 05

will, be going to, can, be able to

1 will + 동사원형 ~할 것이다(미래의 의지 또는 예정)

I **will stay** at home tomorrow. 나는 내일 집에 **머물 것이다.**

① 부정문: will not = won't

It **won't rain** this weekend. 이번 주말에는 **비가 오지 않을 거야.**

② 의문문: Will + 주어 + 동사원형 ~?

Will you **go** to bed at 11? – Yes, I will. / No, I won't.

*Won't로 물으면 권유의 의미로 '~하지 않을래?'가 된다.

2 be going to + 동사원형 ~할 예정이다, ~할 것이다(미래의 예정)

We **are going to fly** to Japan next week.

① 부정문: am/are/is + not going to + 동사원형

She **is not going to call** you again.

② 의문문: Am/Are/Is + 주어 + going to + 동사원형 ~?

Is he **going to visit** you tomorrow? – Yes, he is. / No, he isn't.

He is able to repair this washing machine.

3 can + 동사원형 ~할 수 있다(능력), ~해도 된다(허가)

We **can do** it. / You **can (= may) go** home now.

① 부정문: cannot = can't

I **can't remember** your address.

② 의문문: Can + 주어 + 동사원형 ~?

Can I **use** your bike? – Yes, you can. / No, you can't.

4 be able to + 동사원형 ~할 수 있다

He **is able to repair** this washing machine.

She **will can** cook pasta. (×) / She **will be able to cook** pasta. (○)

PRACTICE

다음 우리말을 영작하시오. (괄호 안에 주어진 단어를 사용할 것)

1 나는 다음 달에 15살이 될 것이다. (fifteen, next month) 상명중 1학년 최근 기출 응용

____

2 세미(Semi)는 자기 고양이를 데려가지 않을 거야. (take, her) 경희여중 1학년 최근 기출 응용

____

3 펭귄들이 날 수 있니? (penguins) 중동중 1학년 최근 기출 응용

____

4 Sam은 3시에 여기에 도착할 수 있을 것이다. (will, arrive, at 3) 상명중 1학년 최근 기출 응용

____

NOW REAL TEST 1

1 다음 우리말에 맞게 빈칸에 알맞은 말을 쓰시오. (미래형을 사용할 것) 사직여중 1학년 최근 기출 응용

이리 오지 않을래?

→ ______________ you ______________ here?

2 다음 우리말을 바르게 영작하시오. 화홍중 1학년 최근 기출 응용

(1) 그녀는 춤을 잘 출 수 있습니까?

→ ______________________________

(2) 그녀는 춤을 잘 출 수 없습니다.

→ ______________________________

3 다음 우리말에 맞게 빈칸에 알맞은 말을 쓰시오. 금오중 1학년 최근 기출 응용

A ⓐ ______________________ badminton tomorrow?
(너 내일 배드민턴 칠 거니?)

B No, ⓑ ______________________.
(아니, 안 칠 거야.)

4 다음 ⓐ와 ⓑ를 어법에 맞게 고쳐 쓰시오. 대흥중 1학년 최근 기출 응용

A ⓐ Can he swims very well?

B ⓑ No, he isn't.

ⓐ ______________________ ⓑ ______________________

5 주어진 단어를 활용하여 다음 문장을 영작하시오. 동성중 1학년 최근 기출 응용

너는 어떤 종류의 음식을 만들 예정이니?

(what kind of, are, going to)

→ ______________________________

NEW WORDS

- kind 종류

6 〈보기〉의 단어와 적절한 조동사를 사용하여 빈칸을 채우시오. 일산동중 1학년 최근 기출 응용

〈보기〉 rain play

(1) It's sunny today, but it ____________ tomorrow.

(2) I can play table tennis, but I ____________ tennis.

7 다음 문장에서 틀린 부분을 찾아 의미가 변하지 않게 고쳐서 문장 전체를 다시 쓰시오. 양운중 1학년 최근 기출 응용

(1) Can Jack does his homework by himself?

→ ________________________________

(2) They will can pass the exam.

→ ________________________________

8 다음 빈칸에 공통으로 들어갈 말을 쓰시오. 개림중 1학년 최근 기출 응용

- I like children very much. I will ________ a good teacher.
- I like this town. I am going to ________ here two weeks more.

9 다음 그림을 보고 Jane이 각 요일에 해야 할 일을 미래형을 사용하여 완성하시오. 동학중 1학년 최근 기출 응용

Wed.	Thurs.	Fri.

Make a Cake	Go Shopping	Watch a Movie

(1) Jane ____________________ on Wednesday.

(2) Jane ____________________ on Thursday.

(3) Jane ____________________ on Friday.

NEW WORDS

□ table tennis 탁구 □ by oneself 스스로, 혼자서 □ pass 합격하다 □ exam 시험 □ children 아이들(child의 복수형)
□ town 도시, 마을

NOW REAL TEST 2

1 주어진 단어 수에 맞도록 다음 우리말을 영작하시오.

(1) 나는 그 자전거를 타지 않을 예정이다. (8단어)

→ ______________________________

(2) 그는 그 무거운 상자를 옮길 수 없다. (9단어)

→ ______________________________

2 다음 글에서 틀린 부분을 모두 찾아 바르게 고치시오.

I have two brothers, John and Jim. John is ten years old, and Jim is eight years old. John can plays soccer well. He will be a soccer player. Jim can't play soccer well. But he can play the piano well. He will can play it much better later. I like both of them very much.

→ ______________________________

____

3 다음은 우주 여행의 마지막 여정을 하고 있는 팀의 대장이 대원들에게 하는 말이다. 빈칸에 be going to, can, will, be able to를 각각 한 번씩만 넣어서 글을 완성하시오.

It's Friday. According to the schedule, we ________ ________ ________ arrive on Saturday. We will ________ ________ ________ see our families soon. We ________ do it! Don't worry! We ________ be great astronauts.

4 다음 문장을 의미가 같은 다른 표현을 사용하여 문장 전체를 다시 쓰시오. (will이나 can을 사용하지 말 것)

(1) He will build a new house on Jeju Island.

→ ______________________________

(2) She can finish the project by tomorrow.

→ ______________________________

NEW WORDS

□ both 둘 다 □ according to ~에 따르면 □ schedule 일정 □ arrive 도착하다 □ soon 곧 □ worry 걱정하다
□ astronaut 우주비행사 □ finish 끝내다 □ project 과제, 프로젝트

UNIT 06

must, should, have to, may

1 must + 동사원형 ~해야 한다(강한 의무)

He **must go** to see a doctor. 그는 병원에 **가야 한다**.

① 부정문: must not + 동사원형 (~하면 안 된다)

You **must not (= mustn't) touch** the painting.
너는 그 그림을 **만져서는 안 된다**.

② 의문문: Must + 주어 + 동사원형 ~?

Must I **wait** for her? – Yes, you must. / No, you mustn't.

2 should[have/has to] + 동사원형 ~해야 한다(당연한 의무)

① should 부정문: should not + 동사원형 (~하면 안 된다)

You **should not (= shouldn't) talk** to her now.
너는 지금 그녀에게 **이야기하면 안 된다**.

② have to 부정문: don't have to[don't need to, need not] + 동사원형 (~할 필요가 없다)

He **doesn't have to pay**. 그는 **돈을 지불할 필요가 없다**.

He must go to see a doctor.

3 may + 동사원형 ~해도 된다(허가), ~일지도 모른다(추측)

You **may go** home. 너는 집에 **가도 된다**.

She **may leave** Seoul soon. 그녀는 곧 서울을 **떠날지도 모른다**.

① 부정문: may not + 동사원형

Exo **may not come** today. 엑소는 오늘 **안 올지도 모른다**.

② 의문문: May + 주어 + 동사원형 ~?

May I **go** to your office now? 지금 당신의 사무실로 **가도 되나요**?

PRACTICE

다음 우리말을 영작하시오. (괄호 안에 주어진 단어를 사용할 것)

1 오후에 비가 많이 올지도 모른다. (it, a lot) 함박중 1학년 최근 기출 응용

____

2 너는 미안하다고 말할 필요가 없다. (don't, say sorry) 신정중 1학년 최근 기출 응용

____

3 우리는 교실에서 조용히 해야 한다. (must) 개금여중 1학년 최근 기출 응용

____

4 디저트를 주문해도 되나요? (order, dessert)

____

NOW REAL TEST 1

1 문맥에 맞도록 빈칸에 알맞은 말을 쓰시오. 효문중 1학년 최근 기출 응용

It's Sunday. Students ____________ ____________ to go to school.

2 다음 그림을 보고, 대화를 완성하시오. 상명중 1학년 최근 기출 응용

A ________________________________? (여기에 주차해도 됩니까?)

B __________, ________________________.

3 다음 우리말을 영어로 옮길 때 빈칸에 알맞은 말을 쓰시오. 연수중 1학년 최근 기출 응용

너는 학교에 늦으면 안 된다.

〈조건〉 should를 꼭 사용할 것

→ You ____________ ____________ ____________ late for school.

4 다음 도서관 규칙을 읽고, 어법상 틀린 곳 2개를 찾아 바르게 고쳐 쓰시오. 배재중 1학년 최근 기출 응용

- You must not make any noise.
- You should return your books in two weeks.
- You should putting trash in the trash can.
- You have turn off your cell phone.

________________________ → ________________________

________________________ → ________________________

NEW WORDS

□ make noise 떠들다 □ return 반납하다 □ trash 쓰레기 □ trash can 쓰레기통 □ turn off 끄다

5 다음 표지판을 보고 should를 사용하여 문장을 완성하시오. 고대부중 1학년 최근 기출 응용

(1) You ______________________________.

(2) You ______________________________.

광희중 1학년 최근 기출 응용

6 다음은 은지가 아버지께 콘서트를 보러 가도 되는지 여쭤보는 대화이다. 빈칸에 알맞은 말을 쓰시오.

은지 Dad, ________ I ________ to the JYP concert?

아버지 No, you ________ ________.

7 주어진 단어를 사용하여 다음 문장을 영어로 바르게 옮기시오. 강일중 1학년 최근 기출 응용

(1) 너는 그 문을 닫아야 한다. (should)

→ ______________________________

(2) 너는 그 문을 닫으면 안 된다. (must)

→ ______________________________

(3) 너는 그 문을 닫을 필요가 없다. (have to)

→ ______________________________

8 다음 글에서 어법상 틀린 부분을 모두 찾아 고쳐서 글 전체를 다시 쓰시오. 금명중 1학년 최근 기출 응용

Seahorse babies can stays in a pouch for a long time. So, an adult seahorse has not to watch its babies all the time.

→ ______________________________

____

NEW WORDS

□ seahorse 해마 □ pouch 주머니 □ for a long time 오랫동안 □ adult 다 자란, 성체의 □ watch 보살피다, 주시하다

NOW REAL TEST 2

1 주어진 단어를 사용하여 다음 우리말을 영어로 옮기시오.

그녀가 당신과 함께 춤을 춰야 하나요? (have to)

→ ______________________________

2 다음 대화의 내용에 맞게 빈칸에 알맞은 말을 한 단어로 쓰시오.

A I don't want to be fat. Can you help me?
B Sure. You ________ eat fast food. And you ________ exercise regularly.

3 다음 글에서 어법상 어색한 곳을 모두 찾아 바르게 고치시오.

What should we do to succeed in the future? First, we have not play computer games too much. And we should going to study hard.

→ ______________________________

____

4 주어진 문장과 비슷한 의미의 문장을 두 개 쓰시오.

She doesn't have to call him back.
= ______________________________
= ______________________________

5 다음 우리말을 바르게 영작하시오.

(1) 그녀는 여기에 안 올지도 모른다.

→ ______________________________

(2) 내가 당신의 차를 운전해도 되나요?

→ ______________________________

NEW WORDS

☐ exercise 운동하다 ☐ regularly 규칙적으로 ☐ succeed 성공하다 ☐ future 미래 ☐ hard 열심히
☐ call ~에게 전화하다

선생님, 헷갈려요!
시험에 잘 나오는 헷갈리는 문제

• **여러 가지 조동사 표현**

must be: ~임이 틀림없다

She **must be** a movie star. 그녀는 영화배우임에 틀림없어.

can't (= cannot) be: ~일 리가 없다

She **can't be** a movie star. 그녀는 영화배우일 리가 없어.

had better + 동사원형: ~하는 게 낫다

You **had better** ask your mom first. 엄마에게 먼저 물어보는 게 좋겠어.

had better not + 동사원형: ~하지 않는 게 낫다

You **had better not** stay any longer. 너는 더 오래 머무르지 않는 게 낫겠어.

확인 문제

1 다음 우리말을 영어로 옮길 때 빈칸에 알맞은 말을 쓰시오.

(1) Tony는 유명한 가수일 리가 없어.

→ Tony ______ ______ a famous singer.

(2) 너 창백해 보여. 더 이상 일하지 않는 게 낫겠어.

→ You look pale. You ______ ______ ______ work anymore.

2 다음 〈보기〉에서 알맞은 표현을 골라 빈칸에 쓰시오.

〈보기〉	had better	must be	can't be	had better not

(1) You look very tired today. You ______ take a rest.

(2) She is very honest. She ______ a liar.

(3) This is a dangerous place. We ______ stay here.

(4) He can play the piano very well. He ______ a good pianist.

(5) She always takes care of the baby. She ______ the baby's mother.

Chapter 4

비교급과 최상급, 감탄문과 명령문

UNIT 07 비교급과 최상급

UNIT 08 감탄문과 명령문

UNIT

07 비교급과 최상급

1 비교급 형용사·부사 + -er / more + 형용사·부사

Your shoes are **dirtier** than my shoes. 너의 신발은 나의 신발보다 **더 더럽다.**

My uncle is **more handsome** than my dad. 삼촌은 아빠보다 **더 잘생겼다.**

2 최상급 the + 형용사·부사 + -est / the most + 형용사·부사

Mt. Halla is **the highest** mountain in South Korea.

She is **the most powerful** woman in the country.

3 불규칙 비교급과 최상급

good - better - best / bad - worse - worst / many, much - more - most / little - less - least / far - farther - farthest (먼) / far - further - furthest (정도가 큰) / late - later - latest (늦은) / late - latter - last (나중의)

Your shoes are dirtier than my shoes.

4 동등 비교

① as + 형용사·부사의 원급 + as: ~만큼 …한

She is **as tall as** her mom. 그녀는 그녀의 엄마**만큼 키가 크다.**

② not as[so] + 형용사·부사의 원급 + as: ~만큼 …한 것은 아닌

Money is **not as valuable as** health. 돈은 건강**만큼 가치 있는 것은 아니다.**

(= Health is more valuable than money.)

③ as ~ as possible = as ~ as + 주어 + can/could: 가능한 한 ~한[하게]

Run **as** fast **as possible**. = Run **as** fast **as you can**. **가능한 한** 빨리 달려라.

5 비교급 강조 표현 a lot, even, still, much, far(훨씬)

He is **very** taller than James. (×)

He is **even** taller than James. (○) 그는 James보다 **훨씬** 키가 크다.

PRACTICE

다음 우리말을 영작하시오. (괄호 안에 주어진 단어를 사용할 것)

1 세계에서 가장 긴 강은 무엇이니? (river, in the world) 목일중 1학년 최근 기출 응용

2 그의 집은 이 집보다 더 비싸다. (this, than, expensive) 목동중 1학년 최근 기출 응용

3 Alice는 보통 그녀의 엄마보다 더 일찍 일어난다. (usually, get up, early) 강현중 1학년 최근 기출 응용

4 시간은 돈만큼 중요하다. (as, time, important) 목동중 1학년 최근 기출 응용

NOW REAL TEST 1

1 주어진 단어를 사용하여 그림 속 인물들을 비교하는 문장을 완성하시오. 백석중 1학년 최근 기출 응용

(1) Yujin is ______________ than Sujin. (tall)

(2) Sujin's hair is ______________ than Yujin's. (short)

2 주어진 단어를 사용하여 아래 그림과 일치하도록 빈칸에 알맞은 말을 쓰시오. 작전중 1학년 최근 기출 응용

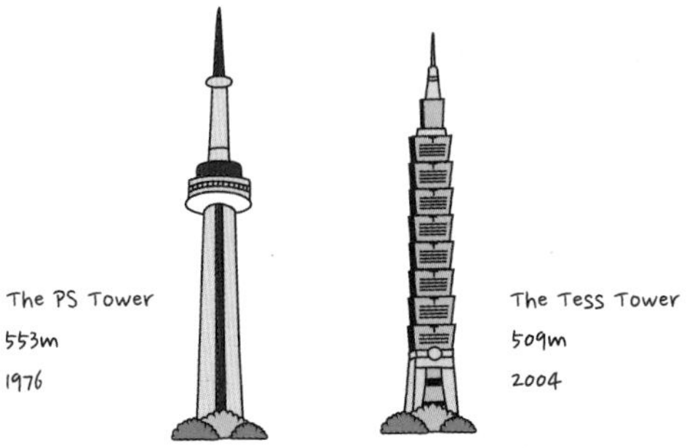

(1) The PS Tower is ______________ ______________ the Tess Tower. (old)

(2) The Tess Tower is ______________ ______________ the PS Tower. (short)

3 다음 중 형용사의 비교급과 최상급을 바르게 쓴 학생은 모두 몇 명인가? 남외중 1학년 최근 기출 응용

이름	원급	비교급	최상급
보검	pretty	more pretty	most pretty
강준	thin	thinner	thinnest
중기	early	more earlier	most earliest
효주	bad	worse	worst
신혜	useful	more useful	most useful

① 1명 ② 2명 ③ 3명 ④ 4명 ⑤ 5명

NEW WORDS

□ thin 얇은, 마른 □ useful 유용한

4 괄호 안의 단어를 사용하여 다음 우리말을 바르게 영작하시오. 성심여중 · 신화중 1학년 최근 기출 응용

(1) 그는 한국에서 가장 인기 있는 가수이다. (popular)

→ ______________________________

(2) 이 소리는 저 음악만큼 크다. (this sound, that music, loud)

→ ______________________________

5 다음은 지현이의 비교급 빙고판이다. 비교급이 잘못 쓰인 것은? 송곡중 1학년 최근 기출 응용

fatter	① more interesting	② louder
softer	③ less	④ bigger
smaller	more difficult	⑤ more cheap

6 다음 글의 내용으로 보아 빈칸에 알맞은 표현을 쓰시오. 광희중 1학년 최근 기출 응용

What animal has __________ __________ teeth? Surprisingly, it is the snail. Its mouth is only as big as the head of a pin, but there are about 20,000 teeth on its tongue.

7 주어진 우리말을 참고하여 ⓐ~ⓒ에 알맞은 말을 쓰시오. 동도중 1학년 최근 기출 응용

- Russia is ⓐ ____________________ in the world. (가장 큰 나라)
- The Maybach Exelero is ⓑ ____________________ in the world. (가장 비싼 차)
- We are ⓒ ____________________ in the world. (가장 행복한 사람들)

8 다음 중 어법상 옳은 것은? 중앙대부속중 1학년 최근 기출 응용

① The sun is biger than the moon.

② This box is heavier than that box.

③ The apples are more expensiver than the bananas.

④ I am taller then my brother.

⑤ She gets up earlyer than Nancy.

NOW REAL TEST 2

1 다음 우리말을 영어로 옮길 때 빈칸에 알맞은 말을 쓰시오.

준영이는 윤기만큼 똑똑하다.

→ Junyeong is ________ ________ ________ Yungi.

2 다음 두 문장의 의미가 같도록 빈칸에 알맞은 말을 쓰시오.

(1) Baseball is more popular than soccer in America.

→ Soccer is ________ ________ popular ________ baseball in America.

(2) I have two sisters, and Jessica has three sisters.

→ Jessica has ________ sisters ________ me.

3 다음 우리말을 바르게 영작하시오.

그것은 그 가게에서 가장 비싼 드레스였다. (it, shop, was)

→ ________________________________

4 다음 중 우리말을 영어로 잘못 옮긴 것을 모두 고르시오.

① 그는 세상에서 가장 재미있는 영화를 봤다. → He saw the most interesting movie in the world.

② John은 Terry보다 훨씬 더 힘이 세다. → John is very stronger than Terry.

③ Jerry는 그의 아빠만큼 키가 크다. → Jerry is as taller as his father.

④ 그 거북이는 가능한 한 빨리 달렸다. → The turtle ran as fast as possible.

⑤ 그녀는 자기 할머니만큼 예쁘지는 않다. → She is not as pretty as her grandmother.

5 다음 표를 보고, 빈칸에 알맞은 말을 쓰시오.

	Sodam	Goeun
Going to Bed	11:00 p.m.	11:30 p.m.
Getting Up	7:30 a.m.	8:00 a.m.

(1) Sodam gets up ________ ________ Goeun.

(2) Goeun sleeps ________ long ________ Sodam.

UNIT 08

감탄문과 명령문

1 What 감탄문 What + a(n) + 형용사 + 명사 (+ S + V)!

It is a very nice car. → **What a nice car it is!** 정말 좋은 차구나!

They are very nice cars. → **What nice cars they are!** 정말 좋은 차들이구나!

2 How 감탄문 How + 형용사 (+ S + V)!

It is a very nice car. → **How nice the car is!** (= How nice it is!)

They are very nice cars. → **How nice the cars are!** (= How nice they are!)

3 명령문(일반동사) 동사원형 ~ / Don't (= Do not) + 동사원형 ~

*Never + 동사원형 ~: 절대 ~하지 마라

Get up early. 일찍 **일어나라**.

Study hard. 열심히 **공부해라**.

Don't fight in the classroom. 교실에서 **싸우지 마라**.

Do not throw garbage on the ground. 쓰레기를 땅에 **버리지 마시오**.

4 명령문(be동사) Be + 형용사 ~ / Don't (= Do not) + be + 형용사 ~

Be quiet. 조용히 해.

Be happy. 행복하렴.

Don't be scared. 겁먹지 마.

Do not be rude to teachers. 선생님들에게 버릇없이 굴지 마라.

5 권유문 Let's + 동사원형 ~ / Let's not + 동사원형 ~

Let's protect our children. 우리 아이들을 **보호하자**.

Let's not stay here anymore. 여기서 더 이상 **머물지 말자**.

What a nice car it is!

PRACTICE

다음 우리말을 영작하시오. (괄호 안에 주어진 단어를 사용할 것)

1 정말 예쁜 컵들이구나! (what) 거제여중 1학년 최근 기출 응용

2 다른 사람들에게 친절해라. (nice, to others) 강북중 1학년 최근 기출 응용

3 창문을 열지 마시오. (the windows) 경암중 1학년 최근 기출 응용

4 너 정말 친절하구나! (how, kind) 문현중 1학년 최근 기출 응용

NOW REAL TEST 1

1 자연스러운 대화가 되도록 빈칸에 알맞은 말을 쓰시오. 개금여중 1학년 최근 기출 응용

Teacher What time is it now, Baekhyeon?
Baekhyeon It's nine o'clock. I'm sorry. I'm late.
Teacher Please, ________ ________ late again.

신목중 1학년 최근 기출 응용

2 다음 대화 중 어색한 문장 2개를 찾아 밑줄을 긋고, 그 문장을 바르게 고쳐 다시 쓰시오.

Sujin Who is the girl in the picture, Jack?
Jack She is my friend, Jasmine.
Sujin How tall girl she is! She looks like a camel.
Jack Don't says that to her. She will be angry.

→ ________________________________

____

재현중 1학년 최근 기출 응용

3 다음은 수업 시간에 지켜야 할 사항이다. 적절하지 않은 표현을 2개 골라 바르게 고쳐 쓰시오.

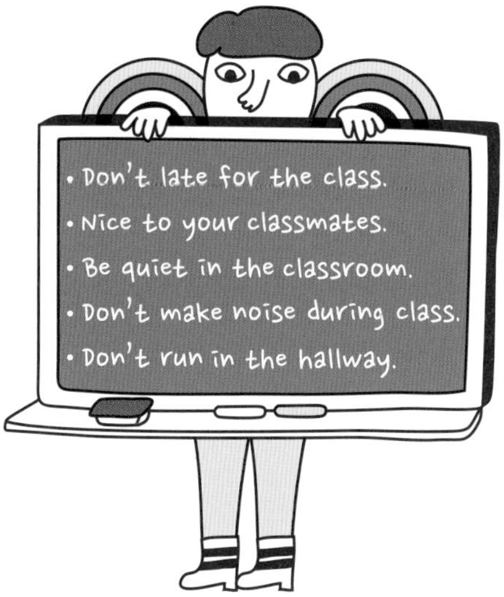

• Don't late for the class.
• Nice to your classmates.
• Be quiet in the classroom.
• Don't make noise during class.
• Don't run in the hallway.

→ ________________________________

____

→ ________________________________

____

4 Tommy는 어제 있었던 하루 일과의 제목을 "아주 행복한 날이었어!"라고 지었다. 제목을 영어로 쓰되, 주어, 동사와 What을 넣어서 감탄문으로 쓰시오. 철산중 1학년 최근 기출 응용

→ ______ ______ ______ ______ ______ ______

NEW WORDS

□ camel 낙타 □ classmate 같은 반 학생 □ hallway 복도

5 주어진 단어를 사용하여 다음 문장을 감탄문으로 바꾸시오. 도농중 1학년 최근 기출 응용

(1) You have a really nice bag.

→ ______________________________ you have! (what)

(2) He is very cute.

→ ______________________________ he is! (how)

6 주어진 단어를 사용하여 밑줄 친 우리말을 바르게 영작하시오. 용호중 1학년 최근 기출 응용

Cover your eyes and walk to the picture. Then, 꼬리에 그림을 붙이세요.

(the tail, the picture, on, put)

→ ______________________________

7 다음 표지판의 내용을 4단어 이상의 명령문으로 쓰시오. 백신중 1학년 최근 기출 응용

새들에게 먹이를 주지 마세요.

→ ______________________________

8 다음 명령문 중 틀린 문장 3개를 골라 바르게 고쳐서 문장 전체를 다시 쓰시오. 능곡중 1학년 최신 기출 응용

ⓐ Be water the plants.
ⓑ Not push the stop button.
ⓒ Got up early.
ⓓ Never take pictures here.
ⓔ Don't be shy.

→ ______________________________

→ ______________________________

→ ______________________________

NEW WORDS

□ tail 꼬리 □ shy 수줍어 하는

NOW REAL TEST 2

[1-3] 주어진 문장을 What 감탄문과 How 감탄문으로 각각 바꾸시오.

1 It is a very nice bike.

(1) What ______________________________!

(2) How ______________________________!

2 They are very old trees.

(1) What ______________________________!

(2) How ______________________________!

3 You are a very smart student.

(1) What ______________________________!

(2) How ______________________________!

4 주어진 표현을 이용해서 부정 명령문을 만드시오.

(1) ______________ in the museum. You can't bring your camera inside. (take pictures)

(2) ______________. You can do better next time. (be disappointed)

5 다음 중 틀린 문장을 모두 고른 것은?

ⓐ What beautiful flower it is!

ⓑ Don't enter the kitchen.

ⓒ How fast the car is!

ⓓ Let's don't go to the hospital.

ⓔ What a amazing view it is!

① ⓐ, ⓓ　② ⓐ, ⓒ, ⓔ　③ ⓐ, ⓓ, ⓔ

④ ⓑ, ⓓ, ⓔ　⑤ ⓓ, ⓔ

NEW WORDS

□ museum 박물관 □ inside 안에 □ next time 다음 번에 □ disappointed 실망한 □ amazing 놀라운, 멋진
□ view 경관, 전망

선생님, 헷갈려요!
시험에 잘 나오는 헷갈리는 문제

• **명령문, and/or ~**

명령문, **and** ~: …해라, 그러면 ~할 것이다

Take this map, **and** you will find the place easily.
= **If** you take this map, you will find the place easily.
이 지도를 가져가라, **그러면** 너는 그 장소를 쉽게 찾을 것이다.

명령문, **or** ~: …해라, 그렇지 않으면 ~할 것이다

Water the flower regularly, **or** it will dry out.
= **If** you **don't** water the flower regularly, it will dry out.
= **Unless** you water the flower regularly, it will dry out.
그 꽃에 규칙적으로 물을 줘라, **그렇지 않으면** 말라버릴 것이다.

확인문제

주어진 단어를 사용하여 빈칸에 알맞은 말을 쓰시오.

(1) 열심히 운동해라, 그러면 너는 훨씬 더 건강해질 것이다. (exercise)
= ______ hard, ______ you will be much healthier.
= ______ you ______ hard, you will be much healthier.

(2) 그녀에게 지금 전화해라, 그렇지 않으면 그녀는 너를 떠날 것이다. (call)
= ______ her now, ______ she will leave you.
= ______ you ______ ______ her now, she will leave you.
= ______ you ______ her now, she will leave you.

(3) 할아버지, 할머니를 자주 찾아뵈어라, 그렇지 않으면 나중에 후회할 것이다. (visit)
= ______ your grandparents often, ______ you will regret it later.
= ______ you ______ ______ your grandparents often, you will regret it later.
= ______ you ______ your grandparents often, you will regret it later.

Chapter 5

전치사와 접속사

UNIT 09

전치사

1 시간, 때를 나타내는 전치사

① in: ~에(월, 계절, 연도, 세기), ~후에(미래)

I first met her **in 2012.** / I will visit you **in October.**

② at: ~에(시각)

I have dinner **at 7 o'clock** every day.

③ on: ~에(날짜, 요일, 특정한 날)

I play soccer **on Saturdays.**

On my birthday, I will invite a lot of friends.

④ 기타: before(~ 전에), after(~ 후에), around(대략 ~에), for(~ 동안 *숫자), during(~ 동안 *특정 기간), until(~까지 *상태 지속), by(~까지 *일이 완료되는 시점)

He played the computer game **for three hours.**

She learned to play the flute **during summer vacation.**

The movie will be over **by** 9. / I stayed there **until** midnight.

She learned to play the flute during summer vacation.

2 장소, 위치를 나타내는 전치사

① at: 일반적 장소, 비교적 작은 장소, 행사나 모임

I am **at home** now. / I met him **at a party.**

② in: 비교적 넓은 장소(도시 이상)

Seo Inguk was born **in Ulsan.**

③ on: ~위에(표면에 닿은 경우), 교통 수단, 통신 수단

There are two books **on the desk.**

④ 기타: over(~ 위에 *표면과 떨어진 경우), under(~ 아래에), in front of(~ 앞에), behind(~ 뒤에), next to(~ 옆에), between(~ 사이에 *둘 사이), among(~ 사이에 *셋 이상), across from(~ 건너편에), near(~ 근처에), around(~ 주위에), across(~을 가로질러)

He was waiting for her **in front of** her house.

PRACTICE

다음 우리말을 영작하시오. (괄호 안에 주어진 단어를 사용할 것)

1 그녀는 방과 후에 무엇을 하니? (what, do) 반포중 1학년 최근 기출 응용

2 많은 학생들이 학교 앞에서 버스를 기다리고 있다. (waiting for the bus, the school) 거제여중 1학년 최근 기출 응용

3 한 남자가 내 옆에서 책을 읽고 있다. (a man, reading) 강북중 1학년최신 기출 응용

4 그 상자들은 그 의자 아래에 있다. (are) 해송중 1학년 최근 기출 응용

NOW REAL TEST 1

1 다음 그림을 보고, 빈칸에 알맞은 전치사를 쓰시오. 도농중 1학년 최근 기출 응용

(1) There is an umbrella __________ the chair.

(2) A dog is sleeping __________ the desk.

(3) There are two books __________ the desk.

2 다음 그림을 보고, 빈칸에 알맞은 전치사를 쓰시오. 홍진중 1학년 최근 기출 응용

→ The hospital is __________ the two high buildings.

3 다음 중 우리말을 영어로 바르게 표현한 것을 모두 고르시오. 북서울중 1학년 최근 기출 응용

① Jane is sitting next at me. (Jane이 내 옆에 앉아 있다.)

② She lives in Seoul. (그녀는 서울에 살고 있다.)

③ A cat is under the table. (고양이 한 마리가 탁자 아래에 있다.)

④ A bird is flying over the tree. (새 한 마리가 나무 위를 날아가고 있다.)

⑤ A deer is among two lions. (사슴 한 마리가 사자 두 마리 사이에 있다.)

NEW WORDS

☐ umbrella 우산 ☐ deer 사슴

4 다음 질문에 대한 답으로 가장 적절한 것은? 용호중 1학년 최근 기출 응용

Sam is next to Jun. Karl is between Min and Jun. Jake is next to Sam. Who is Jake?

① A ② B ③ C ④ D ⑤ E

5 괄호 안에서 알맞은 전치사를 고르시오. 홍진중 1학년 최근 기출 응용

(1) My house is (behind / among) the post office.

(2) Do this homework (near / by) tomorrow.

6 수진이는 자기 방을 꾸몄다. 꽃병(vase) 안에 꽃을 꽂고, 침대 옆에 컴퓨터를 두었다. 이 방의 모습을 표현할 때, 적절한 전치사를 써서 빈칸을 채우시오. 백신중 1학년 최근 기출 응용

(1) There are some flowers ________ ________ ________.

(2) There is a computer ________ ________ ________ ________.

7 다음 우리말을 영어로 옮기시오. (단, 전치사를 각 문장에 사용할 것) 반포중 1학년 최근 기출 응용

(1) 그녀는 세 시간 동안 숙제를 했다.

→ ____________________

(2) 그는 여름방학 동안에 일본어를 배웠다.

→ ____________________

NEW WORDS

□ post office 우체국 □ Japanese 일본어

NOW REAL TEST 2

[1-2] 주어진 질문에 대한 알맞은 대답을 고르시오.

1

A When are you going to the museum?

B ________________.

① At the morning ② In the night ③ In Sunday
④ On Wednesday ⑤ At October

2

A Where are you going to eat the hamburger?

B ________________.

① At Seoul ② On the Internet ③ During lunchtime
④ On the meeting ⑤ In my office

[3-4] 다음 우리말과 같은 뜻이 되도록 빈칸에 알맞은 전치사를 쓰시오.

3

큰 늑대 한 마리가 도로를 가로질러 달리고 있다.

→ A big wolf is running ____________ the street.

4

많은 고양이들이 공원 주위를 걷고 있다.

→ A lot of cats are walking ____________ the park.

5 다음 중 전치사의 쓰임이 적절하지 않은 것은?

① I like getting up early in the morning.
② They live in New York.
③ We learned about Korean history yesterday.
④ I like Picasso just like my mom.
⑤ I usually go to school with bus.

NEW WORDS

□ lunchtime 점심시간 □ wolf 늑대 □ street 거리 □ history 역사

UNIT 10

접속사

When I was young, I was a dancer.

1 등위 접속사 and(그리고), but(그러나), or(또는), so(그래서)

I like pizza **and** chicken. / She loves him, **but** he doesn't love her.

2 시간의 접속사 when(~할 때), before(~하기 전에), after(~한 후에), until(~할 때까지) + S + V

When I was young, I was a dancer. = I was a dancer **when** I was young.

*시간을 나타내는 부사절에서 주절이 미래형이라도 종속절에는 현재형을 써야 한다.

**주절: 주된 문장 / 종속절: 「접속사 + S + V」로 구성된 문장

I will call you **when** I finish my work. (will finish는 틀림)

3 이유의 접속사 because, since, as(~하기 때문에) + S + V

I like IU **because** she sings well. = **Because** she sings well, I like IU.

*because + S + V / because of + 명사구(명사, 대명사, 동명사)

Because he helped me, I was safe. / **Because of** his help, I was safe.

4 조건의 접속사 If(만약) + S + V

I will go there **if** you allow me.

*조건을 나타내는 부사절에서 주절이 미래형이라도 종속절에는 현재형을 써야 한다.

I can do this **if** my boss **gives** me enough time. (will give는 틀림)

5 명사절을 이끄는 접속사 that S + V(주절) + that + S' + V'(종속절)

*주로 believe, think, hope, know, say 등의 동사 뒤에 쓰이며, 목적어절에 쓰인 that은 생략 가능하다.

① 주어(~라는 것은): **That** he came home early is surprising.

② 목적어(~라는 것을): I believe (**that**) I can fly in the sky.

③ 보어(~라는 것이다): The fact is **that** he told me a lie.

PRACTICE

다음 우리말을 영작하시오. (괄호 안에 주어진 단어를 사용할 것)

1 나는 그 그림을 볼 때면 행복하다. (look at, the painting) 중평중 1학년 최근 기출 응용

____

2 Picasso는 그의 친한 친구가 죽은 후에 이 그림을 그렸다. (close friend, make, this painting) 신화중 1학년 최근 기출 응용

____

3 그녀는 똑똑하기 때문에 이 문제를 풀 수 있다. (smart, solve, this question) 목동중 1학년 최근 기출 응용

____

4 우리는 그것이 늑대였다고 생각했다. (wolf, thought, that, it) 서곶중 1학년 최근 기출 응용

____

NOW REAL TEST 1

1 주어진 단어를 모두 사용하여 다음 우리말을 영어로 옮기시오. 중대부속중 1학년 최근 기출 응용

네가 화장실을 가고 싶을 때 손을 들어라.

(hand, go to the restroom, when, your, raise, you, want to)

→ ______________________________

2 우리말과 같은 뜻이 되도록 주어진 단어를 사용하여 문장을 완성하시오. (필요한 단어를 추가할 것) 숭곡중 1학년 최근 기출 응용

(1) 미래에 대해 생각할 때, 어떤 기분이 드나요?

→ ______ ______ ______ ______ the future, how do you feel? (think)

(2) 그는 용감하기 때문에 어떤 두려움도 없다.

→ ______ ______ ______ ______, he doesn't have any fear. (brave)

3 다음 글에서 틀린 부분을 찾아서 바르게 고쳐 쓰시오. 구리여중 1학년 최근 기출 응용

My uncle is going to visit my house this weekend. While he will stay here, I will go to an amusement park with him.

______________ → ______________

4 빈칸에 알맞은 접속사를 쓰시오. 구리여중 1학년 최근 기출 응용

여러분이 여름에 캠핑을 갈 때, 항상 모기를 조심해야 한다는 것을 기억해라.

→ ______ you go camping in summer, remember ______ you should watch out for mosquitoes.

5 다음 문장의 빈칸에 들어갈 말로 알맞은 것은? 광운중 1학년 최근 기출 응용

I think ______ Tom is very smart.

① so ② it ③ but ④ that ⑤ what

NEW WORDS

□ **restroom** 화장실 □ **raise** 들어올리다 □ **fear** 두려움 □ **brave** 용감한 □ **amusement park** 놀이공원
□ **watch out for** ~을 조심하다 □ **mosquito** 모기

계양중 1학년 최근 기출 응용

6 지유는 지훈이에게 "나는 네가 착하기 때문에 네가 좋아."라고 말하려 한다. 빈칸에 알맞은 말을 쓰시오.

Jiyu I like you ________ ________ ________ nice.

Jihun Thank you for saying that.

7 다음 중 어법에 맞게 말한 사람은? 계산여중 1학년 최근 기출 응용

① 효린: She is a doctor is true.

② 수지: The problem is that he has no money.

③ 설현: I will stay there until he will come.

④ 성재: If you will stay here one more day, I will give you a present.

⑤ 기광: When study hard, my mom is happy.

8 다음 빈칸에 공통으로 들어갈 알맞은 말을 쓰시오. 관양중 1학년 최근 기출 응용

- We thought ________ it was a monster.
- He believes ________ he can do it.

9 괄호 안에서 알맞은 것을 고르시오. 관양중 1학년 최근 기출 응용

(1) I know (that / since) she is very energetic.

(2) She will pass the exam if she (will study / studies) hard.

10 다음 밑줄 친 부분 중 생략할 수 있는 것은? 영란여중 1학년 최근 기출 응용

We think(①) that(②) it's(③) an(④) old(⑤) castle.

NEW WORDS

□ doctor 의사, 박사 □ problem 문제 □ present 선물 □ monster 괴물 □ energetic 활동적인 □ castle 성

NOW REAL TEST 2

1 because나 because of를 사용하여 다음 우리말을 바르게 영작하시오.

(1) 그가 그녀를 도왔기 때문에 그녀는 행복했다.

→ ______________________________

(2) 그의 도움 덕분에 그녀는 행복했다.

→ ______________________________

2 적절한 접속사를 사용하여 다음 두 문장을 한 문장으로 만드시오.

It rained yesterday. We didn't go on a picnic.

→ ______________________________

3 〈보기〉에서 알맞은 접속사를 사용하여 다음 두 문장을 한 문장으로 만드시오.

〈보기〉 because until that when but and

(1) He is a famous singer. It is true.

→ ______________________________

(2) He did his best. He failed the exam.

→ ______________________________

4 다음 일기를 읽고, 밑줄 친 ⓐ~ⓔ에서 어색한 곳을 찾아 바르게 고치시오.

I didn't go to school today ⓐ so it was Children's Day. So I went to Lotte World ⓑ with Donghun or Junha. I really enjoyed myself there, ⓒ and Junha didn't ⓓ that he had a stomachache. ⓔ Before we visited Lotte World, we returned home and had dinner together.

ⓐ __________ → __________ ⓑ __________ → __________

ⓒ __________ → __________ ⓓ __________ → __________

ⓔ __________ → __________

NEW WORDS

□ go on a picnic 소풍을 가다 □ fail 실패하다, 떨어지다 □ stomachache 복통 □ return 돌아오다

선생님, 헷갈려요!
시험에 잘 나오는 헷갈리는 문제

• 주의해야 할 전치사

in + 하루의 특정한 때

in the morning 아침에 / in the afternoon 오후에 / in the evening 저녁에

at + 하루의 특정한 때

at noon 정오에 / at night 밤에 / at midnight 자정에 / at dawn 새벽에

• '~ 동안'이라는 의미의 표현

① for + 숫자

He waited for her **for** five hours.

그는 5시간 동안 그녀를 기다렸다.

② during + 특정 기간

We learned Chinese **during** the summer vacation.

우리는 여름방학 동안 중국어를 배웠다.

③ while + S + V (동작)

While you were having lunch, I did my homework.

네가 점심을 먹는 동안에 나는 숙제를 했다.

확인 문제

1 다음 우리말과 같은 뜻이 되도록 괄호 안에서 알맞은 표현을 고르시오.

그는 저녁에 도서관에 있었다.

He was in the library (at evening / in the evening).

2 〈보기〉에서 알맞은 단어를 골라 빈칸에 쓰시오.

〈보기〉 for　　during　　while

(1) He brushed his teeth ________ two minutes.

(2) We played computer games ________ you were sleeping on the sofa.

(3) ________ the long holiday, I will take a rest ________ a week.

Chapter 6

명사, 대명사, 관사

UNIT 11 명사, 대명사

UNIT 12 관사, 부정대명사

UNIT 11

명사, 대명사

1 셀 수 있는 명사

① 보통 명사: 셀 수 있는 사람이나 사물의 이름
I have **a computer**. / He has **two sisters**.

② 집합 명사: 같은 종류의 사람이나 사물이 모인 집합체 (family, group, police 등)

③ 명사의 복수형
대부분의 명사 + **-s**: He has four **sons**.
-ch, -sh, -o, -x, -s + **-es**: There are three **benches**.
자음 + y = y → **i** + **-es**: Her **babies** are very cute.
-f → **-ves**: **Leaves** are falling from the trees.
불규칙: man → men / mouse → mice / child → children / foot → feet / fish → fish / sheep → sheep / deer → deer

He has four sons.

2 셀 수 없는 명사 셀 수 없으므로 무조건 단수 취급한다. (복수 형태가 없음)

① 물질 명사: 일정한 형태가 없는 명사 (money, water, air, salt 등)
② 추상 명사: 추상적 개념을 나타내는 명사 (love, peace, health 등)
③ 고유 명사: 고유한 이름을 나타내는 명사 (Seoul, Korea, Jessica, Paris 등)

3 셀 수 없는 명사의 수량 표현

a cup of coffee / a glass of milk / a piece of furniture / a slice of cheese / a bottle of cola / two cups of tea / three glasses of water / ten sheets of paper / four slices of pizza / many bottles of wine

4 대명사

① 인칭대명사: I, you, he, she, us, her 등
② 지시대명사: this/these, that/those, it, they

PRACTICE

다음 우리말을 영작하시오. (괄호 안에 주어진 단어를 사용할 것)

1 이것들은 내 남동생의 장난감이다. (my brother's, toys) 송호중 1학년 최근 기출 응용

2 나는 작은 마을에 산다. (in, town) 오류중 1학년 최근 기출 응용

3 너는 파란색 가방들을 갖고 있니? (do, have, blue) 부흥중 1학년 최근 기출 응용

4 나의 아버지는 아침에 두 잔의 커피를 마신다. (cups, coffee, in the morning) 신덕중 1학년 최근 기출 응용

NOW REAL TEST 1

1 다음 중 명사의 복수형이 틀린 것은? 탄방중 1학년 최근 기출 응용

① bicycle – bicycles

② wolf – wolves

③ deer – deers

④ key – keys

⑤ woman – women

2 다음 밑줄 친 ⓐ~ⓔ 중 틀린 것을 골라 바르게 고쳐 쓰시오. 내동중 1학년 최근 기출 응용

I have ⓐ a farm. My wife and I grow ⓑ vegetable there. We like to eat ⓒ carrots and ⓓ tomatoes. We have two ⓔ kids. They are cute. I am happy.

________ → ________

3 주어진 우리말에 맞게 빈칸을 영어로 채우시오. 매원중 1학년 최근 기출 응용

Dodo eats ______ ______ ______ ______. (하루에 세 번)

4 밑줄 친 우리말에 맞게 주어진 단어를 활용하여 빈칸에 알맞은 말을 쓰시오. (의미에 맞게 단어를 변형할 것) 태평중 1학년 최근 기출 응용

The monster looks very scary. It also has 강한 이빨들과 커다란 두 눈.

(two, and, eye, strong, tooth, big)

→ It also has ________________.

5 다음 빈칸에 알맞은 단어를 쓰시오. 송라중 1학년 최근 기출 응용

I have a friend. ⓐ ______ name is Cheolsu. He likes soccer. He has a cute sister. ⓑ ______ name is Sujin. She likes drawing.

NEW WORDS

□ farm 농장 □ grow 재배하다 □ vegetable 채소 □ carrot 당근 □ scary 무서운 □ draw 그림을 그리다

6 다음 글에서 밑줄 친 ⓐ~ⓔ 중 틀린 것을 찾아 바르게 고쳐 쓰시오. 진접중 1학년 최근 기출 응용

Some ⓐ animal use their ⓑ tails to rest. Kangaroos sit on ⓒ their tails. ⓓ Foxes cover their ⓔ bodies with their tails.

______ → ______

7 다음 글에서 어법상 어색한 곳 3개를 찾아 바르게 고치시오. 덕이중 1학년 최근 기출 응용

One day, I was very hungry, so I opened my wallet. I found three coin. I went to the market. There were many womans. I bought some cheeses and milk.

______ → ______

______ → ______

______ → ______

8 다음 밑줄 친 부분을 바르게 고쳐 쓰시오. 대화중 1학년 최근 기출 응용

(1) That are my books. → ______

(2) He drank two cup of coffees. → ______

9 다음 우리말을 영어로 바르게 쓰시오. (반드시 복수형을 사용할 것) 세화여중 1학년 최근 기출 응용

그는 약간의 딸기와 감자를 샀다.

→ ______

10 다음 문장을 복수 형태로 다시 쓰시오. 공도중 1학년 최근 기출 응용

(1) This is a very old car.

→ ______

(2) That is my favorite book.

→ ______

NEW WORDS

□ rest 쉬다 □ cover 가리다 □ wallet 지갑 □ coin 동전 □ market 시장 □ favorite 제일 좋아하는

NOW REAL TEST 2

1 다음 중 명사의 복수형이 틀린 것은?

① piano – pianos
② fish – fish
③ wife – wifes
④ box – boxes
⑤ bench – benches

2 다음 우리말을 영어로 바르게 쓰시오.

저 공들은 나의 것이 아니다.

→ ______________________________

3 다음 대화에서 어법상 틀린 부분을 찾아 바르게 고치시오.

A Did you bring your bike?
B No, I didn't bring them. I forgot.

______________ → ______________

4 다음 문장에서 틀린 부분을 찾아 바르게 고쳐 문장을 다시 쓰시오.

(1) He bought me two loaves of breads.

→ ______________________________

(2) I drink a lot of waters a day.

→ ______________________________

5 다음 괄호 안에서 알맞은 것을 고르시오.

(1) David needs ten (sheets / sheet) of paper.

(2) There are several (bar of chocolates / bars of chocolate) on the desk.

NEW WORDS

□ forget 잊어버리다 □ several 몇몇의

UNIT 12

관사, 부정대명사

1 부정관사 a, an 불특정한 명사 앞에 쓰인다.

I have **a** big house. / This is **an** octopus. / She has **an** MP3 player.

2 정관사 the 특정하거나 명확한 명사 앞에 쓰인다.

① 한 번 언급한 것을 가리킬 때

He has a cat. **The** cat is very cute.

② 악기 이름 앞에

She can play **the** guitar very well.

③ 유일한 것을 나타낼 때

The moon is very beautiful tonight.

④ 최상급, 서수 앞에

Seoul is **the** biggest city in Korea.

The moon is very beautiful tonight.

3 무관사 관사가 필요 없는 경우

식사, 스포츠, 교통수단, 본래의 목적으로 쓰이는 장소 등은 무관사로 쓴다.

Sally is having **dinner**.

She likes playing **baseball**.

I go to **school** every day.

4 부정대명사 정해지지 않은 불특정한 대상을 언급한다.

① one: I lost my bike. I need a new **one**.

② ones: I broke my glasses. I need new **ones**.

③ 부정대명사/부정형용사 some, any: '약간, 어떤'의 의미로 some은 긍정문과 권유의 의문문에, any는 부정문과 의문문에 사용된다.

I have **some** money. / I don't have **any** money.

I'm going to make coffee. Would you like **some**?

PRACTICE

다음 우리말을 영작하시오. (괄호 안에 주어진 단어를 사용할 것)

1 Terry는 그의 가방 안에 약간의 치즈를 갖고 있다. (cheese) 원촌중 1학년 최근 기출 응용

____

2 우리 점심을 함께 먹자. (let's, together) 공도중 1학년 최근 기출 응용

____

3 너는 공원에서 몇몇 사람들을 볼 수 있다. (can, in the park) 가락중 1학년 최근 기출 응용

____

4 우리는 지금 농구를 하고 있다. (basketball) 동덕여중 1학년 최근 기출 응용

____

NOW REAL TEST 1

1 다음 빈칸에 공통으로 알맞은 말을 쓰시오. 대전서중 1학년 최신 기출 응용

- Can you play ________ piano?
- You can see ________ moon clearly tonight.

2 다음 대화의 빈칸에 알맞은 말을 쓰시오. 내동중 1학년 최신 기출 응용

A I watched a movie yesterday. ⓐ ________ movie was great.
B How did you go to the movies?
A I went there ⓑ ______________. (버스 타고)

3 다음 중 어법에 맞는 문장이 모두 몇 개인지 쓰시오. 금옥중 1학년 최신 기출 응용

ⓐ The dogs are running in the field.
ⓑ They went to school by the taxi.
ⓒ It's summer! Let's go to sea!
ⓓ Can you pass me the salt?
ⓔ I have any money.

→ ______________

4 다음 빈칸에 가장 알맞은 말은? 신동중 1학년 최근 기출 응용

A I have an old camera. It doesn't work well these days.
B You need to buy a new ________.

① some ② one ③ any
④ it ⑤ that

5 다음 빈칸에 공통으로 들어갈 말을 쓰시오. 문창중 1학년 최근 기출 응용

- ________ Earth moves around ________ sun.
- I saw a dog yesterday. ________ dog was very big.

NEW WORDS

□ clearly 뚜렷하게, 분명하게 □ tonight 오늘 밤에 □ field 들판 □ these days 요즘 □ Earth 지구

6 대화를 읽고 괄호 안에서 알맞은 것을 고르시오. 광희중 1학년 최근 기출 응용

Mom　Hana, hurry up. I will make ⓐ (some / any) fruit juice for you.
Hana　Wow. I will go home ⓑ (by / by a / by the) taxi right now.

7 다음 대화의 빈칸에 공통으로 들어갈 말을 쓰시오. 동도중 1학년 최근 기출 응용

A　Can Boksil play ________ piano well?
B　Yes, she is ________ best pianist in her town.

8 다음 그림을 보고, 상황에 맞는 단어를 〈보기〉에서 골라 빈칸을 채우시오. 신정중 1학년 최근 기출 응용

〈보기〉 some　any　the　a　an　by　one

Waiter　Do you want ⓐ ________ cold water?
Jack　Yes, please. We came here ⓑ ________ bike. It's very hot.
Jane　What is ⓒ ________ most delicious dish here?
Waiter　ⓓ ________ dish is good, but I recommend the cream pasta.
Jack　We'll have two of that ⓔ ________.

NEW WORDS
□ hurry up 서두르다 □ right now 지금 당장 □ delicious 맛있는 □ dish 요리 □ recommend 추천하다

NOW REAL TEST 2

1 다음 우리말과 같은 뜻이 되도록 주어진 단어를 사용하여 문장을 완성하시오.
(단, 필요 없는 단어는 쓰지 말 것)

예쁜 꽃들이 많이 있다. 그 중에서 나는 빨간색 꽃들이 정말 좋다.

(red, I, really, ones, one, some, any, like, the)

→ There are many beautiful flowers. Among them, ______________.

2 다음 우리말과 같은 뜻이 되도록 빈칸에 알맞은 단어를 쓰시오.

이 가방은 조금 작아요. 더 큰 것이 있나요?

→ This bag is a little small. Do you have a bigger ______________?

[3-4] 주어진 단어를 활용하여 다음 우리말을 영작하시오. (단, 필요 없는 단어는 쓰지 말 것)

3 그는 매일 지하철을 타고 집에 간다.

(subway, every day, the, a, by)

→ ______________

4 어제는 봄 학기의 첫날이었다.

(the, day, first, of, semester, spring, a)

→ ______________

5 다음은 민수가 삼촌을 소개하는 글이다. 빈칸 ⓐ~ⓔ에 a, an, the 중 알맞은 것을 쓰시오. (단, 중복 사용 가능하고, 아무것도 안 쓸 때는 '무관사'라고 쓸 것)

My uncle is ⓐ ______ scientist. He works at ⓑ ______ university. When he works, he wears ⓒ ______ uniform. ⓓ ______ uniform's color is white. He goes to work by ⓔ ______ bike. He likes riding his bike.

NEW WORDS

□ subway 지하철 □ semester 학기 □ scientist 과학자 □ university 대학 □ uniform 제복

선생님, 헷갈려요!

시험에 잘 나오는 헷갈리는 문제

• 지시대명사 that과 지시형용사 that

지시대명사 **that**: '저것'으로 해석한다. 말 그대로 대명사이다.

That is my bike. 저것은 나의 자전거이다.

I like **that**. 나는 저것이 좋다.

지시형용사 **that**: '저 ~'라고 해석하며 뒤에 명사가 온다. 말 그대로 형용사이다.

Do you know **that** boy? 너 저 남자애 아니?

• go to school과 go to the school

본래의 목적을 나타낼 때는 관사를 쓰지 않는다.

I **go to school** on foot. 나는 학교에 걸어서 간다.

He **goes to bed** at 11. 그는 11시에 자러 간다.

그 장소에 다른 목적으로 갈 때는 관사를 붙인다.

We **went to the school** to find something. 우리는 뭔가 찾으려고 학교(건물)에 갔다.

I **went to the bed** to fix it. 나는 침대를 고치려고 침대로 갔다.

확인 문제

1 밑줄 친 That[that]이 지시대명사인지 지시형용사인지 쓰시오.

(1) That man is my math teacher. → ____________

(2) That is my favorite book. → ____________

(3) That was not my fault. → ____________

(4) I know that museum. → ____________

2 다음 괄호 안에서 알맞은 표현을 고르시오.

(1) We went to (school / the school) by bus every day last year.

(2) He went to (bed / the bed) to spread a mat.

Chapter 7

형용사와 부사

UNIT 13 형용사

UNIT 14 부사

UNIT 13

형용사

1 형용사의 쓰임과 위치

① 형용사 + 명사: I bought a **beautiful** dress.

② -thing, -body, -one + 형용사: I need something **cold**.
I need cold something. (×)

③ 동사 + 형용사(주격 보어): She is **smart**.

④ 동사 + 목적어 + 형용사(목적격 보어): Danny's voice makes girls **happy**.

2 수량형용사

① many + 셀 수 있는 명사: There were **many people** in the park.

② much + 셀 수 없는 명사: We don't sell **much milk** a day.

*much는 주로 부정문, 의문문에 사용한다. 긍정문에는 a lot of(= lots of)를 사용한다.

**a lot of(= lots of)는 셀 수 있는 명사와 셀 수 없는 명사에 모두 사용 가능하다.

③ few, a few, little, a little

	수 (셀 수 있는 명사)	**양** (셀 수 없는 명사)
조금 있는	a few (복수 취급)	a little
거의 없는 (부정적 의미)	few (복수 취급)	little

There **are a few guests** at the party. 그 파티에 손님들이 **조금 있다**.

There **is little milk** in the bottle. 병 안에 우유가 **거의 없다**.

3 How many + 복수명사 / How much + 단수명사 ~?

How many people are there in the room?

How much money do you have now?

*How + 형용사: 얼마나 ~한 / How + 부사: 얼마나 ~하게

How tall is your father? 너희 아버지는 **얼마나 키가 크시니**?

How fast can Sejin run? 세진이는 **얼마나 빨리** 달릴 수 있니?

I bought a beautiful dress.

PRACTICE

다음 우리말을 영작하시오. (괄호 안에 주어진 단어를 사용할 것)

1 나는 많은 돈을 가지고 있지 않다. (don't have) 성암여중 1학년 최근 기출 응용

____

2 Susan은 방학 동안 책을 거의 읽지 않았다. (not을 사용하지 말 것) 덕포여중 1학년 최근 기출 응용

____

3 우리는 그곳에서 많은 야생 동물들을 봤다. (wild animal, there) 가람중 1학년 최근 기출 응용

____

4 내가 너에게 흥미로운 뭔가를 말해 줄게. (interesting) 양동여중 1학년 최근 기출 응용

____

NOW REAL TEST 1

1 다음 빈칸에 알맞은 말이 순서대로 짝지어진 것은? 연산중 1학년 최근 기출 응용

- How ________ salt do you need?
- I read ________ books in the library.
- There are ________ people in the stadium.

① many – much – many
② much – many – many
③ much – many – much
④ many – many – many
⑤ much – much – much

2 다음 중 many나 much가 어법에 맞게 쓰인 문장을 모두 고르시오. 내성중 1학년 최근 기출 응용

① I have many milk.
② I don't have much books.
③ My sister has many friends.
④ I don't have much water.
⑤ I have much pencils.

3 다음 괄호 안에서 알맞은 표현을 고르시오.

(1) We don't have (many / much) time to waste. 한천중 1학년 최근 기출 응용

(2) How (many / much) hours do you have to do this? 삼천중 1학년 최근 기출 응용

(3) I have (few / little) water to give you. 괴정중 1학년 최근 기출 응용

4 다음 빈칸에 알맞은 말이 순서대로 짝지어진 것은? 천보중 1학년 최근 기출 응용

- We drank ________ coffee yesterday.
- I didn't have ________ time to do it at that time.
- There were ________ soldiers in the battle.

① a lot of – much – few
② much – many – many
③ lots of – little – many
④ little – much – a little
⑤ a few – few – many

NEW WORDS

□ stadium 경기장 □ waste 낭비하다 □ hour 1시간 □ battle 전투

5 어법상 다음 빈칸에 올 수 없는 말은? 구리여중 1학년 최근 기출 응용

He will keep his son ____________.

① warm ② cool ③ safe
④ comfortably ⑤ happy

6 다음 중 어법상 틀린 문장은? 화정중 1학년 최근 기출 응용

① How heavily are the teeth of snails?
② How long is Pinocchio's nose?
③ He has a few cars.
④ Little milk is left.
⑤ How much money do you have?

7 어법상 다음 빈칸에 알맞은 말은? 지도중 1학년 최근 기출 응용

Seolhyeon looks ____________ today.

① prettily ② happily ③ pale
④ beautifully ⑤ sadly

8 어법상 다음 빈칸에 올 수 있는 말끼리 짝지어진 것은? 해운대여중 1학년 최근 기출 응용

There are ____________ places to visit.

① some – lots of
② little – a little
③ few – much
④ a few – a little
⑤ a few – little

NEW WORDS

□ **safe** 안전한 □ **comfortably** 편안하게 □ **be left** 남아 있다 □ **pale** 창백한

NOW REAL TEST 2

1 주어진 단어를 활용하여 그림에 맞는 문장을 쓰시오. (단, not과 필요 없는 단어는 사용하지 말 것)

(there, few, little, many, much, in the bottle)

→ ______________________________

2 다음 중 빈칸에 쓸 수 없는 것은?

I saw ____________ deer in the forest.

① a lot of
② many
③ lots of
④ much
⑤ small

3 다음 우리말과 같은 뜻이 되도록 괄호 안에 주어진 말을 바르게 배열하여 문장을 완성하시오.

Minho는 Sarah를 위해 특별한 무엇인가를 준비했다.

→ Minho ____________________ for Sarah. (special, prepared, something)

NEW WORDS

□ bottle 병 □ forest 숲 □ prepare 준비하다 □ special 특별한

4 다음 중 어법상 틀린 문장을 모두 고르시오.

① We have lots of homework to do today.

② How many bread do they sell in the bakery?

③ He doesn't have much salt to add to the soup.

④ Is there strange anything here?

⑤ How much milk does your brother drink?

5 다음 우리말과 일치하도록 빈칸에 알맞은 말을 쓰시오.

(1) 그는 쉴 시간이 거의 없었다.

→ He had ________ ________ to rest.

(2) 그는 새 차에 많은 돈을 썼다.

→ He spent ________ ________ ________ ________ on a new car.

NEW WORDS

□ bakery 빵집 □ add 더하다, 첨가하다 □ strange 이상한 □ rest 쉬다 □ spend (시간이나 돈을) 쓰다

UNIT

14 부사

1 부사

① 부사의 의미: '~하게'

② 부사의 역할

동사 수식: The car stopped **suddenly** to pick her up.

형용사 수식: The weather in Texas was **too** hot last summer.

부사 수식: She showed me the way to the hospital **very** kindly.

문장 전체 수식: **Unfortunately**, he failed the exam again.

③ 형태: 일반적으로 '형용사 + ly'

형용사와 부사가 같은 형태: fast, hard, early, late

'형용사 + ly'가 뜻이 다른 경우: hardly(거의 ~ 않는), lately(최근에), nearly(거의), highly(상당히)

The weather in Texas was too hot last summer.

2 빈도부사

① 종류: always, usually, often, sometimes, hardly (ever), rarely, seldom, never

② 위치: be동사·조동사 뒤, 일반동사 앞, 문장의 맨 앞이나 맨 뒤

My English teacher Joy is **always** happy.

I would **sometimes** go to Everland to have fun.

He **never** walks to school.

We have to drink water **often**.

PRACTICE

다음 우리말을 영작하시오. (괄호 안에 주어진 단어를 사용할 것)

1 Steve는 보통 아침 7시에 일어난다. (get up, at 7 a.m.) 동아중 1학년 최근 기출 응용

2 몽실이는 최근에 잠을 잘 자지 못한다. (Mongsil, well) 삼산중 1학년 최근 기출 응용

3 나중에, 그는 최초의 아시아인 비행사가 되었다. (first Asian pilot, later) 양강중 1학년 최근 기출 응용

4 Michael은 오늘 해야 할 많은 숙제가 있다. (to do, today) 세화여중 1학년 최근 기출 응용

NOW REAL TEST 1

1 다음 문장에서 often이 들어가기에 가장 알맞은 곳은? 서초중 1학년 최근 기출 응용

① He ② drives ③ his car ④ to ⑤ the beach.

2 다음 우리말에 맞게 주어진 단어를 바르게 배열하시오.

(1) 나는 항상 비행기 조종사가 되길 원했었어. (I, to be, wanted, a pilot, always) 서운중 1학년 최근 기출 응용

→ ______________________________

(2) 그는 결코 수학에 흥미가 있지 않았다. (he, math, was, interested in, never) 반안중 1학년 최근 기출 응용

→ ______________________________

3 다음 중 어법상 어색한 문장은? 괴정중 1학년 최근 기출 응용

① The game is always played in winter.
② They never will do it again.
③ He usually plays soccer on Sundays.
④ Jane sometimes goes to the sea.
⑤ We often ride our bikes in the park on weekends.

4 다음 중 어법에 틀리게 말한 사람은 누구인지 쓰고, 그 이유를 기술하시오. 덕화중 1학년 최근 기출 응용

효린 My uncle works usually until late. (삼촌은 주로 늦게까지 일하신다.)
보라 They could sometimes go there. (그들은 가끔 거기에 갈 수 있었다.)

→ ______________________________

5 다음 문장을 부정문으로 바꾸시오. (반드시 never를 사용할 것)

(1) You will get bored when you are with me.

→ ______________________________

(2) He does many things for me.

→ ______________________________

NEW WORDS

□ beach 해변 □ be interested in ~에 흥미가 있다 □ bored 지루해 하는

6 주어진 단어를 사용하여 다음 우리말을 영작하시오. 신남중 1학년 최근 기출 응용

(1) 그녀는 그녀의 꿈을 포기했다. (give up)

→ ______________________________

(2) 그녀는 그녀의 꿈을 절대 포기하지 않았다. (give up, never)

→ ______________________________

[7–8] 다음 우리말을 어법에 맞게 영어로 옮긴 것을 고르시오.

금사중 1학년 최근 기출 응용

7 Jake는 숙제를 거의 하지 않는다.

① Jake never does his homework.
② Jake does never his homework.
③ Jake seldom does his homework.
④ Jake sometimes does his homework.
⑤ Jake does hardly his homework.

가산중 1학년 최근 기출 응용

8 그는 종종 그녀에게 친절하다.

① He sometimes be kind to her.
② He is sometimes kind to her.
③ He often be kind to her.
④ He is often kind to her.
⑤ He usually kind to her.

9 다음 우리말을 어법에 맞게 영작하시오. (주어진 단어를 사용하되 필요하면 형태를 바꿀 것) 세마중 1학년 최근 기출 응용

(1) 그들은 가끔 영화를 보러 간다. (go to the movies)

→ ______________________________

(2) 그들은 항상 집 안에 있다. (be, in the house)

→ ______________________________

NEW WORDS

□ give up 포기하다

NOW REAL TEST 2

1 〈보기〉와 같이 주어진 문장을 같은 의미의 다른 문장으로 바꾸어 쓰시오.

〈보기〉 Jason is a quick learner.
→ Jason learns quickly.

Sally is a careless driver.

→ ______________________________

2 괄호 안에서 알맞은 표현을 고르시오.

(1) 그는 매우 높게 점프할 수 있다.

→ He can jump very (high / highly).

(2) 그들은 매우 늦게 서울역에 도착했다.

→ They arrived at Seoul Station very (late / lately).

3 다음 중 밑줄 친 단어의 쓰임이 나머지 넷과 다른 하나는?

① It rained hard yesterday.
② She really works hard every day.
③ They studied very hard for two hours.
④ It was very hard to understand at first.
⑤ He tried hard to win a gold medal.

NEW WORDS

□ quick 빠른 □ quickly 빨리 □ careless 부주의한 □ understand 이해하다

4 다음 중 어법에 맞는 문장은?

① Amy usually can swim in the pool for more than two hours a day.

② Judy often goes to the zoo with her family.

③ They never are late for school.

④ He sometimes visit his uncle when he has free time.

⑤ Sam does seldom the dishes instead of his mom.

5 Tom과 Sean이 컴퓨터 게임을 하는 요일을 나타낸 다음 표를 보고, 적절한 빈도부사를 사용하여 문장을 완성하시오.

	Mon.	Tue.	Wed.	Thurs.	Fri.	Sat.	Sun.
Tom	○	○	○	○	○	○	○
Sean	×	×	×	×	×	×	×

How often do Tom and Sean play computer games?

(1) Tom ______________ computer games.

(2) Sean ______________ computer games.

NEW WORDS

□ more than ~이 넘게 □ do the dishes 설거지하다

선생님, 헷갈려요!
시험에 잘 나오는 헷갈리는 문제

• **감정을 나타내는 형용사로 쓰이는 현재분사(-ing)와 과거분사(p.p.)**

사람이 감정을 느끼는 주체일 때: p.p.(과거분사) 사용

I was very **interested** in the game. 나는 그 경기에 매우 흥미가 있었다.

사물이 감정을 유발하는 주체일 때: -ing(현재분사) 사용

The game was very **interesting**. 그 경기는 매우 흥미로웠다.

확인 문제

1 다음 괄호 안에서 알맞은 것을 고르시오.

(1) I don't want to watch (boring / bored) movies.

(2) We were very (surprising / surprised) by the news.

(3) This kind of game is very (tiring / tired). I won't play it because I don't want to be (tiring / tired).

2 다음 글에서 틀린 부분을 찾아 바르게 고쳐서 글 전체를 다시 쓰시오.

> I watched a fantastic movie about baseball. The movie was very interested. My friend Jesse watched a different movie. It was bored. Jesse was really disappointing by the movie.

→ ______________________________

____

____

Chapter 8

부가의문문, 비인칭주어, 4형식 문장

UNIT 15

부가의문문, 비인칭주어

1 부가의문문

① 평서문은 다음과 같이 부가의문문을 만든다.
긍정 → 부정 / 부정 → 긍정 / 명사 → 대명사 / be동사 → be동사 / 조동사 → 조동사 / 일반동사 → do/does/did
You cannot see bacteria, **can you?**
Yuna bought some books yesterday, **didn't she?**
Mike was sick yesterday, **wasn't he?**
Tom and Jerry aren't good friends, **are they?**

② 명령문은 will you?를 붙이고, Let's로 시작하는 청유문은 shall we?를 붙인다.
Don't be late for school, **will you?**
Let's play soccer, **shall we?**

Yuna bought some books yesterday, didn't she?

2 비인칭주어 it

날씨, 날짜, 요일, 시간, 거리, 명암 등을 나타낼 때 쓰는 주어로, '그것'이라고 해석하지 않는다.
It is snowing a lot. (날씨)
What day is **it** today? (요일)
It takes five hours from Seoul to Busan. (거리)
It is dark outside. (명암)
*지시대명사 it은 '그것'으로 해석한다.
How much is **it**? – **It** is 20 dollars.
그것은 얼마입니까? – 그건 20달러입니다.

PRACTICE

다음 우리말을 영작하시오. (괄호 안에 주어진 단어를 사용할 것)

1 Billy는 쌍둥이 형제가 있어. 그렇지 않니? (twin brother) 서경중 1학년 최근 기출 응용

____

2 커피를 너무 많이 마시지 마라, 알겠니? (drink too much) 덕현중 1학년 최근 기출 응용

____

3 일본은 지금 무슨 계절이니? (what season, in) 상명중 1학년 최근 기출 응용

____

4 공원까지 자전거로 5분이 걸린다. (take, to the park, by) 대영중 1학년 최근 기출 응용

____

NOW REAL TEST 1

1 다음 빈칸에 공통으로 들어갈 알맞은 말을 쓰시오. 지산중 1학년 최근 기출 응용

- ______ is raining cats and dogs now.
- A Who broke the window?
  B ______ was not my fault.

2 다음 문장에서 틀린 부분을 찾아 바르게 고쳐 쓰시오. 숭문중 1학년 최근 기출 응용

That's very dark here. I can't read this book.

______ → ______

3 괄호 안에 주어진 표현을 활용하여 질문에 알맞은 대답을 쓰시오. 고명중 1학년 최근 기출 응용

(1) How long does it take from Seoul to Daegu by KTX? (two hours)

→ ______

(2) How much is this coat? (100 dollars)

→ ______

4 다음 빈칸에 알맞은 부가의문문을 쓰시오.

(1) Your favorite food is fried chicken, ______? 덕명여중 1학년 최근 기출 응용

(2) David and Leo live in New York, ______? 동래중 1학년 최근 기출 응용

(3) Let's do it right now, ______? 신남중 1학년 최근 기출 응용

5 다음 중 밑줄 친 It[it]의 용법이 다른 하나는? 휘경여중 1학년 최근 기출 응용

① It's a very old car.
② How long does it take to Gwangju by car?
③ What day is it today?
④ It's very dark here.
⑤ It's Sunday today.

NEW WORDS

□ rain cats and dogs 폭우가 내리다 □ fault 잘못 □ chicken 닭고기

6 다음 대화의 ⓐ와 ⓑ에 들어갈 말이 바르게 짝지어진 것은? 대전태평중 1학년 최근 기출 응용

A My name is Ashley. I just moved here.
B Nice to meet you. Welcome to TH Town. You came here from SY Town, ___ⓐ___?
A Yes. You don't know SY Town very well, ___ⓑ___?

	ⓐ		ⓑ
①	were you	–	do you
②	didn't you	–	do you
③	did you	–	do you
④	didn't you	–	don't you
⑤	weren't you	–	don't you

7 다음 문장의 부가의문문에 어울리도록 빈칸에 적절한 표현을 써서 문장을 완성하시오. (단, 주어진 단어를 반드시 사용할 것) 상현중 1학년 최근 기출 응용

(1) ______________________, are you? (hungry)

(2) ______________________, doesn't she? (like shopping)

(3) ______________________, shall we? (go to the amusement park)

8 다음 중 밑줄 친 It[it]의 용법이 주어진 문장과 같은 것은? 능인중 1학년 최근 기출 응용

This is a very special dress. Many people wanted to buy it.

① It's almost winter.
② How long does it take from here?
③ Is it bright in your room?
④ How much is it?
⑤ Is it Monday today?

NEW WORDS
□ move 이사하다 □ almost 거의

NOW REAL TEST 2

1 다음은 날씨에 대해 Minho와 Jinhi가 이야기하는 모습이다. 대화의 빈칸에 알맞은 말을 쓰시오.

Jinhi ________ ________ raining outside?

Minho Yes, ________ ________.

2 다음 중 부가의문문이 바르게 쓰인 것은?

① Mansour has a lot of money, isn't he?
② Usain Bolt is the best sprinter, isn't Usain Bolt?
③ Nam Juhyeok is a very good actor, is he?
④ Let's go shopping, shall we?
⑤ Don't let him go, do you?

3 우리말과 같은 뜻이 되도록 괄호 안의 단어를 바르게 배열하시오.

(1) 너는 영화 보는 것에 흥미가 있지 않아, 그렇지?
(you, watching movies, aren't, interested in, are, you)

→ ________________________________

(2) John은 많은 책을 가지고 있었어, 그렇지 않니? (John, a lot of, didn't, books, had, he)

→ ________________________________

NEW WORDS

□ outside 밖에 □ sprinter 단거리 육상선수 □ actor 배우

4 다음 중 밑줄 친 It[it]의 용법이 다른 하나는?

① It is your book.

② Nobody knew it.

③ I will pick it up.

④ It takes five hours to Daejeon.

⑤ It's not my fault.

5 다음 대화에서 어법상 어색한 부분 3개를 찾아 바르게 고쳐 쓰시오.

A How is the weather today?

B This is rainy, but there will be sunny in the afternoon.

A Good. Let's walk to the park in the afternoon, will we?

B That's a good idea.

__________ → __________

__________ → __________

__________ → __________

NEW WORDS

□ nobody 아무도 □ pick up 집어 들다, (맡긴 것을) 찾다 □ weather 날씨 □ rainy 비가 오는 □ sunny 맑은

UNIT 16

4형식 문장

1 4형식 주어 + 동사 + 간접목적어(~에게) + 직접목적어(…을)

4형식 문장에 쓰인 동사는 '~에게 …을 준다'라는 의미의 동사로 수여동사라고 한다.

She **gave** me a nice pen. 그녀는 나에게 좋은 펜을 주었다.

He **sent** me a letter. 그는 나에게 편지를 보냈다.

2 3형식 주어 + 동사 + 목적어 (+ 부사구)

Many people like him. 많은 사람들이 그를 좋아한다.

3 4형식의 3형식으로의 전환

주어 + 동사 + 간접목적어(~에게) + 직접목적어(…을)

→ 주어 + 동사 + 직접목적어 + 전치사 + 간접목적어

① to: 일반적으로 사용됨

Mom gave me a bike.

→ Mom **gave** a bike **to** me.

② for: buy, get, make, cook, choose, find

He bought me a car.

→ He **bought** a car **for** me.

③ of: ask

The teacher asked us a question.

→ The teacher **asked** a question **of** us.

Mom gave me a bike.

PRACTICE

다음 우리말을 영작하시오. (괄호 안에 주어진 단어를 사용할 것)

1 내가 너에게 새 시계를 사 줄게. (will, watch) 숭문중 1학년 최근 기출 응용

2 부모님들은 자녀들에게 사랑을 준다. (give, love, their children) 성사중 1학년 최근 기출 응용

3 나의 삼촌이 나에게 드레스를 만들어 주셨다. (uncle, a dress) 서일중 1학년 최근 기출 응용

4 그녀의 미소는 나에게 행복을 가져다 준다. (smile, happiness, bring) 상명중 1학년 최근 기출 응용

NOW REAL TEST 1

1 다음 문장을 4형식은 3형식으로, 3형식은 4형식으로 바꾸어 쓰시오.

(1) They bought their parents a good car. 국사봉중 1학년 최근 기출 응용

→ ______________________

(2) The teacher showed us a painting. 까치울중 1학년 최근 기출 응용

→ ______________________

(3) He gave some big help to the children. 개림중 1학년 최근 기출 응용

→ ______________________

(4) I will buy your friends some snacks. 동백중 1학년 최근 기출 응용

→ ______________________

(5) My sister cooked me dinner. 매현중 1학년 최근 기출 응용

→ ______________________

(6) The doctor gave some medicine to him. 동수원중 1학년 최근 기출 응용

→ ______________________

(7) I will make my son a delicious cake tomorrow. 대덕중 1학년 최근 기출 응용

→ ______________________

(8) He sent her a gift. 석천중 1학년 최근 기출 응용

→ ______________________

(9) Give all of your clothes to others. 연현중 1학년 최근 기출 응용

→ ______________________

(10) My father made the birds a nest. 한국글로벌중 1학년 최근 기출 응용

→ ______________________

NEW WORDS

□ painting 그림 □ medicine 약 □ gift 선물 □ nest 둥지

2 〈보기〉를 참고하여 두 문장의 의미가 같도록 주어진 문장을 바꾸어 쓰시오. 거원중 1학년 최근 기출 응용

〈보기〉 I will give Dad a belt.
→ I will give a belt to Dad.

My mom will buy him a pair of shoes.

→ My mom will ______________________________.

동수원중 1학년 최근 기출 응용

3 다음은 Gary가 지효(Jihyo)에게 사 줄 것의 목록이다. 괄호 안의 지시대로 빈칸에 알맞은 말을 쓰시오.

〈목록〉 a beautiful bag, a nice car

(1) Gary will buy ______________________. (a beautiful bag / 4형식)

(2) Gary will buy ______________________. (a nice car / 3형식)

4 다음 중 어법상 틀린 것은? 중원중 1학년 최근 기출 응용

① She gave me a present.
② They bought a good car for their son.
③ She cooked some delicious food for us.
④ He lent his new car to his girlfriend.
⑤ Jane asked a question to her teacher.

숭곡중 1학년 최근 기출 응용

5 〈A〉에서 알맞은 단어를 하나씩 선택하여 〈B〉의 빈칸을 채우시오. (필요하면 어형을 바꿀 것)

A will play cook dance can give sing to for

B • Today is my mom's birthday. I will ________ some flowers ________ her.
• My mom always ________ delicious food ________ me.

NEW WORDS
□ lend 빌려주다 □ girlfriend 여자친구

NOW REAL TEST 2

1 다음 빈칸에 알맞은 말을 각각 쓰시오.

- Tom taught English ______________ us last year.
- She bought a new MP3 player ______________ me.
- David asked a good question ______________ us.

[2-3] 다음 우리말을 4형식과 3형식 문장으로 영작하시오.

2 그 남자는 그녀에게 꽃을 주었다. (a flower)

(1) 4형식: ______________________________

(2) 3형식: ______________________________

3 그 회사는 그에게 새 차를 사 주었다. (company)

(1) 4형식: ______________________________

(2) 3형식: ______________________________

4 다음 중 어법상 틀린 문장을 모두 고르시오.

① I made a strong chair to her.

② The boy gave a banana to the monkey in the zoo.

③ My teacher asked an easy question to me.

④ The chef cooked some Italian food for us.

⑤ She will send an email to me.

NEW WORDS

□ company 회사 □ chef 요리사 □ Italian 이탈리아의

5 다음 Nick의 생일 파티 장면을 보고, 친구들이 Nick에게 준 것들을 묘사하는 문장을 완성하시오.

(1) David gave ____________________ Nick.

(2) Roy made ____________________ Nick.

6 다음 표를 바탕으로 은수의 일기를 완성하시오. (단, 각 빈칸에는 한 개의 단어만 쓸 것)

Who?	How?	What?
father	bought	a bag
mother	made	yummy cookies
brother	gave	a doll

<Eunsu's diary>

Saturday, March 7

Today is my birthday. I got a lot of things from my family.

My father ⓐ ________ ________ ________ ________.

My mother ⓑ ________ ________ ________ ________ ________.

And my brother ⓒ ________ ________ ________ ________.

NEW WORDS

□ yummy 맛있는

선생님, 헷갈려요!
시험에 잘 나오는 헷갈리는 문제

• it의 기본적인 쓰임

지시대명사: **'그것'이라고 해석함**

It is an important game. 그것은 중요한 경기이다.

비인칭주어: **시간, 거리, 날짜, 날씨, 명암, 요일, 계절 등에 쓰임. ('그것'이라고 해석하지 않음)**

It gets dark early in the winter. 겨울에는 일찍 어두워진다.

It's Sunday. Let's go to church. 일요일이다. 교회에 가자.

가주어: **주어가 길 때 문장 처음에 가짜로 세우는 주어 ('그것'이라고 해석하지 않음)**

It's very difficult to solve this math question.
이 수학 문제를 푸는 것은 매우 어렵다.

확인 문제

1 다음 중 밑줄 친 It[it]의 쓰임이 나머지와 다른 하나는?

① Is it your cell phone?

② It was a fantastic concert.

③ Where was it?

④ It was really hot yesterday.

⑤ Was it delicious?

2 다음 중 밑줄 친 It[it]의 쓰임이 〈보기〉와 같은 것은?

〈보기〉 How long does it take to the station?

① It looks like a bear.

② It's five o'clock.

③ It is easy to do my homework on the computer.

④ It is very small.

⑤ Is it his laptop?

Chapter 9

to부정사와 동명사

UNIT 17 to부정사

UNIT 18 동명사

UNIT
17 to부정사

1 to부정사의 형태 to + 동사원형

2 to부정사의 명사적 용법 주어, 목적어, 보어의 역할

① 주어(~하는 것은): **To live** without water is impossible.

*가주어 - 진주어: It is impossible to live without water.

② 목적어(~하는 것을): I decided **to go** to Hong Kong next week.

*to부정사를 목적어로 취하는 동사: want, decide, hope, promise, wish, expect, plan 등
(미래의 바람, 희망, 약속, 계획 등의 의미)

**to부정사 또는 동명사를 목적어로 취하는 동사: like, love, hate, begin, start, continue 등

She likes **to clean** her stone collection.

③ 의문사 + to부정사: how/when/where/what + to부정사

I don't know **where to go**. = I don't know **where I should go**.

④ 보어(~하는 것이다): My dream is **to be** an astronaut.

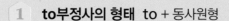

She likes to clean her stone collection.

3 to부정사의 부사적 용법 감정의 원인, 목적, 결과, 판단의 근거, 정도

① 감정의 원인(~해서): He was very pleased **to see** Jane again.

② 목적(~하기 위해): She practiced the piano hard **to join** the music club.

③ 결과(~하게 되다): He awoke **to find** himself famous.

④ 판단의 근거(~하는 것을 보니): He must be brave **to protect** them from the enemies.

⑤ 정도(~하기에는): He is too young **to live** alone.

4 to부정사의 부정 not/never to + 동사원형

Be careful **not to get** lost.

I told him **never to tell** a lie again.

PRACTICE

다음 우리말을 영작하시오. (괄호 안에 주어진 단어를 사용할 것)

1 나는 의사가 되기를 원한다. (be) 중계중 1학년 최근 기출 응용

2 Mr. Smith는 그녀를 기쁘게 하기 위해 노래를 불렀다. (sing, please) 정신여중 1학년 최근 기출 응용

3 아이들과 함께 요리하는 것은 재미있다. (fun, cook) 봉영여중 1학년 최근 기출 응용

4 우리는 약간의 도넛을 사기 위해 줄을 섰다. (line up, some doughnuts) 상명중 1학년 최근 기출 응용

NOW REAL TEST 1

1 다음 우리말을 'to+동사원형'을 사용하여 영작하시오. 태랑중 1학년 최근 기출 응용

그녀의 꿈은 영화 감독이 되는 것이다. (movie director)

→ ______________________

2 다음 우리말에 맞게 빈칸을 채우시오. 숭의여중 1학년 최근 기출 응용

그는 버스를 타기 위해 버스 정류장에 서 있다. (take)

→ He is standing at the bus stop ________ ________ a bus.

3 다음 주어진 단어를 어순에 맞게 재배열하시오. 옥현중 1학년 최근 기출 응용

my mom / me / to / her / help / wanted

→ ______________________

4 우리말과 의미가 같도록 〈보기〉에 주어진 단어를 배열하여 문장을 완성하시오. 작전중 1학년 최근 기출 응용

〈보기〉 the secret, to, tell

너는 그 비밀을 말하기를 원하니?

→ Do you want ______________________?

5 다음 두 문장을 한 문장으로 바꾸시오. 노은중 1학년 최근 기출 응용

(1) I turned on the fan. I wanted to get some cool air.

→ ______________________

(2) He reads a lot of books. He wants to get useful information from them.

→ ______________________

NEW WORDS

□ movie director 영화 감독 □ bus stop 버스 정류장 □ secret 비밀 □ turn on ~을 켜다 □ fan 선풍기
□ useful 유용한 □ information 정보

6 사진을 찍는 목적을 설명하려고 한다. 다음 조건에 맞게 문장을 완성하시오. 매현중 1학년 최근 기출 응용

〈조건 1〉 to부정사를 반드시 사용할 것
〈조건 2〉 7단어 이상으로 쓸 것
〈조건 3〉 주어진 단어를 모두 사용할 것

(my, own, take pictures, make, album)

→ I ______________________________.

7 다음 조건에 맞게 우리말을 영어로 옮기시오. 태랑중 1학년 최근 기출 응용

〈조건〉 'to+동사원형' 형태를 사용할 것

(1) Steve의 꿈은 훌륭한 과학자가 되는 것이다.

→ ______________________________

(2) 나는 여기에 남아 있기를 원한다.

→ ______________________________

8 다음 문장에서 어법상 틀린 곳이 있으면 바르게 고쳐 문장 전체를 다시 쓰고, 없으면 동그라미 표시를 하시오. 강동중 1학년 최근 기출 응용

(1) I don't want watch TV all day long.

→ ______________________________

(2) I really hope seeing her soon.

→ ______________________________

9 다음 '나'의 다짐 중 빈칸 ⓐ와 ⓑ에 목적을 나타내는 알맞은 말을 쓰시오. 백석중 1학년 최근 기출 응용

〈조건〉 'to+동사원형'을 포함하여 쓸 것

I will study hard ⓐ ______________________. (pass, exam)
I will get up early ⓑ ______________________. (late for school)

NEW WORDS

□ **own** 자신의, 직접 ~한

NOW REAL TEST 2

1 다음 그림을 보고, 두 사람의 상황에 맞게 빈칸을 채우시오.

(1) Tom의 상황 (가주어 사용 금지)

→ ________ solve math questions ________ very ________.

(2) Jack의 상황 (가주어 사용할 것)

→ ________ is easy for Jack ________ study English.

2 다음 밑줄 친 ⓐ~ⓔ 중 틀린 부분 2개를 찾아서 바르게 고쳐 쓰시오.

It's Friday. I like ⓐ go to a restaurant with my family ⓑ on Fridays. ⓒ Have dinner with my family ⓓ makes me happy. I ⓔ love my family.

________________ → ________________

________________ → ________________

3 다음 중 어법상 올바른 문장은?

① I hope to go there with you.

② I am happy see you.

③ To not sleep is not good for your health.

④ It was very surprising run into her on the street.

⑤ I study hard get good grades.

NEW WORDS

□ surprising 놀라운 □ run into ~와 마주치다 □ grade 성적, 점수

4 다음 각 문장을 해석하고, 그 중 to부정사의 용법이 나머지 넷과 다른 것을 쓰시오.

(1) I'm very glad to see you again.

→ ____________________

(2) I earn money to buy a new bike.

→ ____________________

(3) It is not easy to collect old newspapers.

→ ____________________

(4) Joyce grew up to be a writer.

→ ____________________

(5) You are very selfish to do such a thing.

→ ____________________

다른 것: __________

5 다음 우리말을 영어로 가장 바르게 표현한 것은?

나의 바람은 누구에게도 무례하게 굴지 않는 것이다.

① My desire is to not be rude to anyone.
② My desire is not be rude to anyone.
③ My desire is to do not be rude to anyone.
④ My desire is not to be rude to anyone.
⑤ My desire is being not rude to anyone.

NEW WORDS

□ earn 벌다 □ collect 모으다 □ writer 작가 □ selfish 이기적인 □ such 그러한 □ desire 바람, 소망 □ rude 무례한

UNIT 18

동명사

1 동명사의 형태 동사 + -ing

2 동명사의 쓰임

① 주어: '~하는 것은'으로 해석 (단수 취급)

Keeping a diary every day **is** not easy. 매일 일기를 쓰는 것은 쉽지 않다.

② 동사의 목적어: '~하는 것을'로 해석

He **enjoys playing** soccer on weekends.

They didn't **mind working** long hours.

He finally **finished repairing** the car.

*동명사를 목적어로 취하는 동사: enjoy, avoid, deny, finish, give up, practice, keep, mind 등

③ 전치사의 목적어: 전치사의 목적어로 동사가 올 때 동명사를 쓴다.

I'm interested **in cooking**.

④ 보어: '~하는 것(이다)'으로 해석

My hobby is **collecting** action figures.

3 동명사와 to부정사를 모두 목적어로 취하는 동사

like, love, hate, begin, start, continue 등의 동사는 동명사와 to부정사 모두 올 수 있다.

I **like eating** pizza. = I **like to eat** pizza.

It **started raining**. = It **started to rain**.

PRACTICE

괄호 안의 단어를 사용하여 다음 우리말을 영작하시오. (동명사를 사용할 것)

1 내 취미는 여가 시간에 축구를 하는 것이다. (in my free time, play) 동아중 1학년 최근 기출 응용

2 더러운 차를 세차하는 것은 매우 어렵다. (wash, cars, hard, is) 서원중 1학년 최근 기출 응용

3 그들은 그 비밀의 방에 들어가는 것을 피했다. (avoid, the secret room, enter) 신사중 1학년 최근 기출 응용

4 이 파티에 저를 초대해 주셔서 감사합니다. (thank you, for, invite, to) 서초중 1학년 최근 기출 응용

NOW REAL TEST 1

1 다음 편지글을 읽고, 밑줄 친 (가)와 (나)를 알맞은 형태로 쓰시오. 대평중 1학년 최근 기출 응용

Hi, Alex. How are you? I hope everything is okay. Thank you for (가) send me a novel last week. I tried to finish (나) read it, but I couldn't because I was busy.

(가) ____________

(나) ____________

2 아래의 단어를 모두 사용하여 '우리는 숙제 하는 것을 빨리 끝내야 한다.'라는 문장을 영어로 옮기시오. (단, 필요하면 단어의 형태를 바꿀 것) 국사봉중 1학년 최근 기출 응용

finish, we, should, our homework, do, soon

→ ____________

3 다음 문장을 영어로 바르게 옮기시오. (what과 watch를 사용할 것) 경원중 1학년 최근 기출 응용

이번 주 토요일에 영화 보는 거 어때?

→ ____________

4 다음 대화에서 어법에 맞지 않는 문장 2개를 찾아 바르게 고치시오. 방배중 1학년 최근 기출 응용

A Look! Brian is playing the piano there.
B Wow, he plays it so well!
A Yes. He is also good at play the violin.
B Wonderful! Is he interested in sing, too?
A Well, he is not a good singer.

____________ → ____________

____________ → ____________

NEW WORDS

□ novel 소설 □ wonderful 대단한, 훌륭한 □ be interested in ~에 흥미가 있다

5 우리말과 같은 뜻이 되도록 괄호 안에 주어진 단어를 사용하여 빈칸에 알맞은 말을 쓰시오. 영일중 1학년 최근 기출 응용

캐나다에 가기 위해 돈을 모으는 것은 내겐 매우 힘들었다. (save)

→ ________ ________ to go to Canada ________ very hard to me.

6 다음 그림을 보고, 상황에 맞게 빈칸을 채우시오. (finish와 wash를 반드시 사용할 것) 광희중 1학년 최근 기출 응용

Sally wants to ________ ________ the dishes as soon as possible.

7 다음 밑줄 친 ⓐ를 바르게 고친 것은? 경암중 1학년 최근 기출 응용

He worked very hard all day long. He stopped ⓐ dig because he was so tired.

① to dig ② digging ③ to digging ④ digs ⑤ dug

8 다음 중 어법상 틀린 문장은? 사직여중 1학년 최근 기출 응용

① Feeding pets is very fun.
② I like sleeping on the sofa.
③ She began working hard after the event.
④ She is good at play the piano.
⑤ My hobby is visiting old cities.

NEW WORDS

□ save 저축하다 □ dig (땅을) 파다 □ tired 피곤한 □ event 사건

NOW REAL TEST 2

1 다음 문장의 괄호 안에 주어진 단어를 알맞은 형태로 쓰시오.

(1) He is interested in (collect) stamps.

→ ______________

(2) I am good at (play) tennis.

→ ______________

(3) We enjoy (read) comic books at the library.

→ ______________

2 주어진 단어를 사용하여 다음 우리말을 영작하시오. (필요하면 어형을 바꾸거나 단어를 추가 사용할 것)

(1) 저를 B1A4의 콘서트에 초대해 주셔서 감사합니다.

(thank you, invite, for, me, to, B1A4's concert)

→ ______________________________

(2) 내가 제일 좋아하는 활동은 동물들의 사진을 찍는 것이다. (to부정사 사용 금지)

(favorite, my, take, picture, activity)

→ ______________________________

3 다음 빈칸에 들어갈 말이 순서대로 바르게 짝지어진 것은?

• I don't mind __________ the window in summer.
• Do you enjoy __________ in the river?

① opening – swimming
② open – to swim
③ opening – to fish
④ to open – fishing
⑤ to open – to fish

NEW WORDS

□ stamp 우표 □ invite 초대하다 □ fish 낚시하다

4 다음 중 어법상 틀린 부분을 바르게 고친 것을 모두 고르시오.

① Matt is good at play soccer. (play → playing)

② He decided going to Japan. (going → go)

③ I was interested in read comic books. (read → to read)

④ He gave up to wait for her. (to wait → waiting)

⑤ Study hard is very difficult. (Study → Studying 또는 To study)

5 다음 표는 반 친구들이 좋아하는 것들을 나타낸 것이다. 표에 나와 있는 정보와 일치하도록 문장을 완성하시오.

	Sam	Harold	Eugene
Play Computer Games	○		
Play Soccer		○	
Read Books	○	○	
Take Naps			○

(1) ______________ is Eugene favorite thing to do. (동명사를 사용할 것)

(2) Sam enjoys ______________ and ______________.

(3) Harold enjoys ______________ and ______________.

6 주어진 단어를 모두 활용하여 다음 우리말을 영작하시오. (단, 필요하면 어형을 바꿀 것)

그는 그 야구 경기를 보는 것에 흥미가 있다.

(he, the baseball game, watch, be interested in)

→ ______________

NEW WORDS

□ decide 결심하다 □ take a nap 낮잠을 자다

선생님, 헷갈려요!
시험에 잘 나오는 헷갈리는 문제

- **to부정사와 동명사 중 뒤에 어떤 것이 오는지에 따라 의미가 달라지는 동사들**

remember + to부정사: **~할 것을 기억하다(미래의 일)**
I **remember to meet** her next week. 나는 다음 주에 그녀를 만날 것을 기억한다.

remember + 동명사(-ing): **~했던 것을 기억하다(과거의 일)**
Do you **remember eating** this before? 이거 전에 먹었던 것을 기억하니?

forget + to부정사: **~할 것을 잊어버리다(미래의 일)**
Don't **forget to turn off** the light before you leave the house.
집을 나서기 전에 불을 끄는 것을 잊지 마라. (아직 안 껐음)

forget + 동명사(-ing): **~했던 것을 잊어버리다(과거의 일)**
I **forgot locking** the door. 나는 문을 잠근 것을 잊어버렸다. (문을 이미 잠갔음)

stop + to부정사: **~하기 위해 멈추다**
He **stopped to call** her. 그는 그녀에게 전화를 하기 위해 멈췄다.

stop + 동명사(-ing): **~하는 것을 멈추다**
He **stopped sending** her letters. 그는 그녀에게 편지 보내는 것을 멈췄다.

try + to부정사: **~하려고 노력하다**
He **tried to enter** the university. 그는 그 대학교에 들어가려고 노력했다.

try + 동명사(-ing): **시험 삼아 ~해보다**
She **tried entering** the room. 그녀는 그 방에 한번[시험 삼아] 들어가 봤다.

확인 문제

1 괄호 안에서 알맞은 것을 고르시오.

(1) He remembers (to buy / buying) her a new bike tomorrow.

(2) She stopped (to give / giving) a beggar some money on the street. Then, she hurried to go to work.

2 다음 우리말을 영어로 옮길 때 괄호 안에서 알맞은 것을 고르시오.

(1) 그는 그 건물을 올려다보기 위해 멈췄다.

→ He stopped (to look up / looking up) at the building.

(2) 그녀는 지난주에 그를 만났던 것을 잊어버렸다.

→ She forgot (to see / seeing) him last week.

memo

memo

쓰담쓰담

내신영문법

1

정답 및 해설

Chapter 1
동사의 현재형

UNIT 01
be동사의 현재형

PRACTICE p. 010

1 The table is in front of the sofa. (또는 The table is in front of a sofa.)
2 Is your uncle a teacher?
3 Kate is shy.
4 There are two cats in the box.

NOW REAL TEST 1 p. 011

1 He is not very kind.
2 Today is her first day at a Korean middle school.
3 ②
해설 ①, ③, ④, ⑤에는 are가, ②에는 is가 들어가야 한다.
4 ④
5 ①
6 My friend Jongin and I are good friends. We are in the same class. Our teachers are very kind.
7 is
8 ⓐ Is Sera riding a bike? ⓑ She is doing her homework.
9 It is small and white.

NOW REAL TEST 2 p. 013

1 ⓐ are ⓑ is ⓒ is ⓓ isn't ⓔ is ⓕ are
2 The girls are listening to music in the classroom.
3 (1) is watching
(2) is drinking (또는 is having)
(3) are playing
4 (1) Is → Are
(2) are → is
(3) They are → She is
5 (1) What is Jimmy doing?
(2) She is watering the plants in the garden.
6 Everything is ready, and many guests is coming. → Everything is ready, and many guests are coming. / There is many good dancers in our school. → There are many good dancers in our school. / Jeongmin and Minjeong is good at dancing. → Jeongmin and Minjeong are good at dancing.

UNIT 02
일반동사의 현재형

PRACTICE p. 015

1 He goes to bed late.
2 I don't go to school by bike.
3 Does she go jogging every morning?
4 Some animals don't use their tails.

NOW REAL TEST 1 p. 016

1 (1) has (2) goes (3) doesn't
2 ③
해설 주어가 They이므로 doesn't가 아니라 don't가 되어야 한다.
3 to
해설 We don't go to school on Sundays.
4 ②
해설 동사가 gets이므로 3인칭 단수가 주어로 와야 한다. ②는 복수이므로 올 수 없다.
5 ③
해설 washes → wash
6 ②
해설 ① go → goes ③ don't → doesn't ④ doesn't → don't ⑤ stops → stop
7 Haeyeong has a dog, but Dogyeong doesn't have a dog.
8 (1) like, likes (2) cook
9 ②
해설 ②에는 Does가 들어가야 하고, 나머지는 Do가 들어가야 한다.
10 A: Do they live in Canada?
B: No, they don't.

NOW REAL TEST 2 p. 018

1 (1) Yes, he does.
(2) No, she doesn't.
2 (1) Brian doesn't go to the movies once a month.
(2) Does Sally clean her room every day?
3 He likes music. He plays the piano well. He often goes to classical music concerts with his friends.
4 (1) Yes, she does.
(2) No, she doesn't. (She teaches English)
5 On Friday, Suji cleans the living room, washes the dishes, feeds the dog, and waters the flowers. But she doesn't clean the bathroom on that day.

선생님, 헷갈려요! p. 020

1 ③ (Look → Look at 또는 Look after)
2 (1) passing (2) like (3) up (4) after

Chapter 2
동사의 과거형

UNIT 03
be동사의 과거형

PRACTICE p. 022

1 I was very ill last year.
2 There were many people in the park.
3 Were you at the YG concert yesterday?
4 The question wasn't (= was not) very difficult.

NOW REAL TEST 1 p. 023

1 Kim Yuna was skating on the ice.
2 I was playing tennis last night.
3 ①
해설 주어가 He and I이므로 was가 아니라 were가 맞다.
4 ②
해설 ②는 was, 나머지는 were가 들어가야 한다.
5 He was playing basketball.
6 A woman was tasting *kimchi* next to me.
7 ④
해설 ① were → was ② was → were ③ were → was ⑤ were → was
8 He was riding a bike.
9 ③
해설 be동사로 물었으므로 be동사로 답해야 한다.
10 ⑤
해설 '~하고 있었다'는 과거진행형을 사용하여 표현한다.

NOW REAL TEST 2 p. 026

1 (1) was doing his homework / was taking care of his younger brother
(2) wasn't cleaning his room / wasn't washing the dishes
2 When I was watching a *pansori* performance, my mom was making rice cakes.
3 (가) I was at the library. (또는 I was in the library.)
(나) I was reading some science books. (또는 I was reading a few science books.)
4 Q: Were there many lions at the zoo?
A: Yes, there were four lions (there).

UNIT 04
일반동사의 과거형

PRACTICE p. 028

1 Molly ran around the house.
2 He didn't get up early today.
3 My parents drank a lot of coffee yesterday.
4 Hodong didn't eat meat for dinner.

NOW REAL TEST 1 p. 029

1 (1) had (2) go (3) didn't buy
2 ③
3 didn't get up
4 My math teacher didn't come to school today.
5 ④
해설 sleep의 과거형은 slept이다.
6 (1) played tennis (2) saw a movie (3) ate out
7 (1) watched TV / watered the plants
(2) didn't eat breakfast / didn't meet my friends
8 ⓐ Did ⓑ he didn't ⓒ Did ⓓ he did
9 (1) ate (2) didn't play
10 (1) went (2) got (3) moved

NOW REAL TEST 2 p. 032

1 visit → visited / feed → fed / jump → jumped / have → had
2 (1) They wanted to go to Jeju.
(2) My father bought groceries at the supermarket.
(3) She cut the cake into two pieces.
3 (1) The bird flew high to the sky yesterday.
(3) He grew a lot of flowers in his garden last summer.
4 (1) Did he send an email to her last night?
(2) Paul and Emma didn't fix the broken machine.
5 A: Did the Korean War break out in 1951?
B: No, it didn't. It broke out in 1950.

Chapter 3
조동사

UNIT 05
will, be going to, can, be able to

PRACTICE p. 036

1 I will be fifteen (years old) next month.
(또는 I am going to be fifteen (years old) next month.)

2 Semi won't (= will not) take her cat.
(또는 Semi isn't (= is not) going to take her cat.)

3 Can penguins fly? (또는 Are penguins able to fly?)

4 Sam will be able to arrive here at 3.

NOW REAL TEST 1 p. 037

1 Won't, come

2 (1) Can she dance well?
(또는 Is she able to dance well?)
(2) She can't dance well.
(또는 She is not able to dance well.)

3 ⓐ Will you play (또는 Are you going to play)
ⓑ I won't (또는 I'm not)

4 ⓐ Can he swim very well?
ⓑ No, he can't.

5 What kind of food are you going to cook?
(또는 What kind of food are you going to make?)

6 (1) will rain (또는 is going to rain)
(2) can't play

7 (1) Can Jack do his homework by himself?
(2) They will be able to pass the exam.

8 be

9 (1) will make a cake (또는 is going to make a cake)
(2) will go shopping (또는 is going to go shopping)
(3) will watch a movie
(또는 is going to watch a movie)

NOW REAL TEST 2 p. 039

1 (1) I am not going to ride the bike.
(2) He is not able to carry the heavy box.

2 John can plays soccer well. → John can play soccer well. / He will can play it much better later. → He will (be able to) play it much better later.

3 It's Friday. According to the schedule, we are going to arrive on Saturday. We will be able to see our families soon. We can do it! Don't worry! We will be great astronauts.

4 (1) He is going to build a new house on Jeju Island.
(2) She is able to finish the project by tomorrow.

UNIT 06
must, should, have to, may

PRACTICE p. 040

1 It may rain a lot in the afternoon.

2 You don't have to say sorry. (또는 You don't need to say sorry.)

3 We must be quiet in the classroom.

4 May (= Can) I order dessert?

NOW REAL TEST 1 p. 041

1 don't have (또는 don't need)

2 A: May I park here? (= Can I park here?)
B: No, you may not.
(또는 No, you should not. / No, you shouldn't. / No, you must not. / No, you mustn't. / No, you cannot. / No, you can't.)

3 should not be

4 You should putting trash in the trash can. → You should put trash in the trash can. / You have turn off your cell phone. → You have to turn off your cell phone.

5 (1) should stop
(2) should not (= shouldn't) ride a bike (ride your bike도 가능)

6 은지: Dad, may (= can) I go to the JYP concert?
아버지: No, you may not.

7 (1) You should close the door.
(2) You must not (= mustn't) close the door.
(3) You don't have to close the door.

8 Seahorse babies can stay in a pouch for a long time. So, an adult seahorse doesn't have to watch its babies all the time.
해설 can 뒤에 동사원형이 와야 하고, '~할 필요가 없다'는 의미의 조동사는 has not to가 아니라 doesn't have to이다.

NOW REAL TEST 2 p. 043

1 Does she have to dance with you?

2 shouldn't (= mustn't), should (= must)

3 We have not play computer games too much. → We should not play computer games too much. / we should going to study hard → we should study hard

4 She doesn't need to call him back. / She needs not call him back.

5 (1) She may not come here.
(2) May (= Can) I drive your car?

선생님, 헷갈려요! p. 044

1 (1) can't (= cannot) be (2) had better not

2 (1) had better (2) can't be (3) had better not
(4) must be (5) must be

Chapter 4

비교급과 최상급, 감탄문과 명령문

UNIT 07
비교급과 최상급

PRACTICE p. 046

1 What is the longest river in the world?

2 His house is more expensive than this house.

3 Alice usually gets up earlier than her mother.

4 Time is as important as money.

NOW REAL TEST 1 p. 047

1 (1) taller (2) shorter

2 (1) older than (2) shorter than

3 ③
해설 강준, 효주, 신혜가 바르게 썼다. 보검이는 pretty – prettier – prettiest로 써야 하고, 중기는 early – earlier – earliest로 써야 한다.

4 (1) He is the most popular singer in Korea.
(2) This sound is as loud as that music.

5 ⑤
해설 cheaper가 되어야 한다.

6 the most
해설 the most는 many의 최상급으로 '가장 많은'의 의미이다.

7 ⓐ the biggest (= largest) country
ⓑ the most expensive car
ⓒ the happiest people

8 ②
해설 ① biger → bigger ③ expensiver → expensive ④ then → than ⑤ earlyer → earlier

NOW REAL TEST 2 p. 049

1 as smart as

2 (1) Soccer is not as[so] popular as baseball in America.
(2) Jessica has more sisters than me.
해설 (2)에서 more는 many의 비교급으로 '더 많은'이라는 의미이다.

3 It was the most expensive dress in the shop.

4 ②, ③
해설 ② 비교급 강조 표현은 very가 아니라 a lot, even, still, much, far 등을 써야 한다. ③ 동등 비교는 as와 as 사이에 원급을 써야 한다. (taller → tall)

5 (1) Sodam gets up earlier than Goeun.
(2) Goeun sleeps as long as Sodam.

UNIT 08
감탄문과 명령문

PRACTICE p. 050

1 What pretty cups (they are)!

2 Be nice to others.

3 Don't (= Do not) open the windows.

4 How kind you are!

NOW REAL TEST 1 p. 051

1 don't be

2 How tall girl she is! → What a tall girl she is! (또는 How tall she is!) / Don't says that to her. → Don't say that to her.

3 Don't late for the class. → Don't be late for the class. / Nice to your classmates. → Be nice to your classmates.

4 What a happy day it was!

5 (1) What a nice bag (2) How cute

6 put the picture on the tail

7 Don't (= Do not) feed the birds.

8 ⓐ Water the plants.
ⓑ Don't (= Do not) push the stop button.
ⓒ Get up early.

NOW REAL TEST 2 p. 053

1 (1) a nice bike it is
(2) nice the bike is
해설 주어와 동사를 생략해서 (1) What a nice bike! (2) How nice!로 써도 된다.

2 (1) old trees they are
(2) old the trees are

해설 주어와 동사를 생략해서 (1) What old trees! (2) How old!로 써도 된다.

3 (1) a smart student you are

(2) smart you are

해설 주어와 동사를 생략해서 (1) What a smart student! (2) How smart!로 써도 된다.

4 (1) Don't take pictures

(2) Don't be disappointed

5 ③

해설 ⓐ What a beautiful flower it is! ⓓ Let's not go to the hospital. ⓔ What an amazing view it is!

선생님, 헷갈려요! p. 054

(1) Exercise hard, and you will be much healthier.
If you exercise hard, you will be much healthier.

(2) Call her now, or she will leave you.
If you don't call her now, she will leave you.
Unless you call her now, she will leave you.

(3) Visit your grandparents often, or you will regret it later.
If you don't visit your grandparents often, you will regret it later.
Unless you visit your grandparents often, you will regret it later.

Chapter 5
전치사와 접속사

UNIT 09
전치사

PRACTICE p. 056

1 What does she do after school?

2 Many (= A lot of) students are waiting for the bus in front of the school.

3 A man is reading a book next to me.

4 The boxes are under the chair.

NOW REAL TEST 1 p. 057

1 (1) next to (또는 by) (2) under (3) on

2 between

3 ②, ③, ④

해설 ① next at → next to ⑤ among → between

4 ⑤

5 (1) behind (2) by

6 (1) in the vase

(2) next to the bed

7 (1) She did her homework for three hours.

(2) He learned Japanese during (the) summer vacation.

NOW REAL TEST 2 p. 059

1 ④

2 ⑤

3 across

4 around

5 ⑤

해설 with bus → by bus

UNIT 10
접속사

PRACTICE p. 060

1 When I look at the painting, I am happy. (또는 I am happy when I look at the painting.)

2 Picasso made this painting after his close friend died. (또는 After his close friend died, Picasso made this painting.)

3 Because (= Since, As) she is smart, she can solve this question. (또는 She can solve this question because (= since, as) she is smart.)

4 We thought (that) it was a wolf.

NOW REAL TEST 1 p. 061

1 When you want to go to the restroom, raise your hand. (또는 Raise your hand when you want to go to the restroom.)

2 (1) When you think about

(2) Because (= Since, As) he is brave

3 will stay → stays

4 When you go camping in summer, remember that you should watch out for mosquitoes.

5 ④

6 because (= since, as) you are

7 ②

해설 ① That she is a doctor is true. ③ I will stay there until he comes. ④ If you stay here one more day, I will give you a present. ⑤ When I study hard, my mom is happy.

8 that

9 (1) that (2) studies

10 ②

NOW REAL TEST 2 p. 063

1 (1) Because he helped her, she was happy. (또는 She was happy because he helped her.)
(2) Because of his help, she was happy. (또는 She was happy because of his help.)

2 Because (= Since, As) it rained yesterday, we didn't go on a picnic. (또는 We didn't go on a picnic because (= since, as) it rained yesterday.)

3 (1) That he is a famous singer is true. (또는 It is true that he is a famous singer.)
(2) He did his best, but he failed the exam.

4 ⓐ so → because (= since, as) ⓑ or → and ⓒ and → but ⓓ that → because (= since, as) ⓔ Before → After

해설 ⓐ 어린이날이기 때문에 학교에 안 간 것이다. ⓑ 동훈이와 준하 둘 다 함께 갔기 때문에 and가 맞다. ⓒ 나는 즐거웠지만 준하는 그렇지 못했다는 내용이 되어야 하므로 but이 적절하다. ⓓ 준하는 배탈이 났기 때문에 즐기지 못했다. ⓔ 롯데월드를 방문한 후에 집에 돌아와 저녁을 먹었다.

선생님, 헷갈려요! p. 064

1 in the evening
2 (1) for
(2) while
(3) During, for

Chapter 6
명사, 대명사, 관사

UNIT 11
명사, 대명사

PRACTICE p. 066

1 These are my brother's toys.
2 I live in a small town.
3 Do you have blue bags?
4 My father drinks two cups of coffee in the morning.

NOW REAL TEST 1 p. 067

1 ③
해설 deer는 단·복수형이 동일하게 deer이다.

2 ⓑ vegetable → vegetables

3 three times a day

4 strong teeth and two big eyes

5 ⓐ His ⓑ Her

6 ⓐ animal → animals

7 coin → coins / womans → women / cheeses → cheese

8 (1) Those
(2) cups of coffee

9 He bought some strawberries and potatoes.

10 (1) These are very old cars.
(2) Those are my favorite books.

NOW REAL TEST 2 p. 069

1 ③
해설 wife의 복수형은 wives이다.

2 Those balls are not mine.

3 them → it

4 (1) He bought me two loaves of bread.
(2) I drink a lot of water a day.

5 (1) sheets
(2) bars of chocolate

UNIT 12
관사, 부정대명사

PRACTICE p. 070

1 Terry has some cheese in his bag.
2 Let's have (= eat) lunch together.
3 You can see some people in the park.
4 We are playing basketball now.

NOW REAL TEST 1 p. 071

1 the

2 ⓐ The ⓑ by bus

3 2개
해설 어법에 맞는 문장은 ⓐ과 ⓓ이다. ⓑ by the taxi → by taxi ⓒ sea → the sea ⓔ any → some (또는 any → no, have → don't have)

4 ②

5 The[the]

6 ⓐ some ⓑ by

7 the

8 ⓐ some ⓑ by ⓒ the ⓓ Any ⓔ one

NOW REAL TEST 2 p.073

1 I really like the red ones

2 one

3 He goes home by subway every day.

4 Yesterday was the first day of the spring semester.

5 ⓐ a ⓑ a ⓒ a ⓓ The ⓔ 무관사

해설 ⓑ, ⓒ university와 uniform의 u가 자음 발음이므로 an이 아니라 a를 써야 한다. ⓓ uniform이 앞에서 한 번 언급되었으므로 정관사 the를 쓴다. ⓔ 교통수단 앞에는 관사를 쓰지 않는다.

선생님, 헷갈려요! p.074

1 (1) 지시형용사 (2) 지시대명사 (3) 지시대명사 (4) 지시형용사

2 (1) school (2) the bed

Chapter 7
형용사와 부사

UNIT 13
형용사

PRACTICE p.076

1 I don't have much (= a lot of, lots of) money.

2 Susan read few books during (the) vacation.

3 We saw many (= a lot of, lots of) wild animals there.

4 I will tell you something interesting.

NOW REAL TEST 1 p.077

1 ②

2 ③, ④

해설 ① milk는 셀 수 없는 명사이므로 much나 a lot of를 쓴다. ② book은 셀 수 있는 명사이므로 many나 a lot of를 쓴다. ⑤ pencil은 셀 수 있는 명사이므로 many나 a lot of를 쓴다.

3 (1) much (2) many (3) little

4 ①

해설 a lot of는 셀 수 있는 명사와 셀 수 없는 명사 모두 가능 / time은 셀 수 없는 명사이고 부정문이므로 much 가능 / soldier는 셀 수 있는 명사이므로 few 가능

5 ④

해설 5형식 문장의 목적격 보어로 부사는 올 수 없다.

6 ①

해설 How heavy are the teeth of snails?가 맞다.

7 ③

해설 2형식 문장에서 감각동사 look의 주격 보어로 부사가 올 수 없으므로 형용사인 pale이 정답이다.

8 ①

해설 place가 셀 수 있는 명사이므로 셀 수 있는 명사에 쓸 수 있는 수량형용사만으로 이루어진 ①이 정답이다.

NOW REAL TEST 2 p.079

1 There is little milk in the bottle.

2 ④

3 prepared something special

4 ②, ④

해설 ② bread는 셀 수 없는 명사이므로 How much가 맞다. ④ strange anything이 아니라 anything strange가 맞다.

5 (1) little time

(2) a lot of money

UNIT 14
부사

PRACTICE p.081

1 Steve usually gets up at 7 a.m.

2 Mongsil doesn't sleep well lately.
(또는 Lately, Mongsil doesn't sleep well.)

3 Later, he became the first Asian pilot.

4 Michael has a lot of (= lots of) homework to do today.

NOW REAL TEST 1 p.082

1 ②

해설 빈도부사 often은 일반동사 drives 앞에 위치해야 한다.

2 (1) I always wanted to be a pilot.

(2) He was never interested in math.

해설 (1) 빈도부사 always가 일반동사 wanted 앞에 위치 **(2)** 빈도부사 never가 be동사 was 뒤에 위치

3 ②

해설 빈도부사 never는 조동사 will 뒤에 위치해야 한다. 따라서 will never do가 되어야 한다.

4 효린, 빈도부사 usually는 일반동사 앞에 위치해야 하므로 usually가 works 앞에 와야 한다.

5 (1) You will never get bored when you are with me.

(2) He never does many things for me.

해설 (1) 빈도부사 never가 조동사 will 뒤에 위치 (2) 빈도부사 never가 일반동사 does 앞에 위치

6 (1) She gave up her dream.
(2) She never gave up her dream.
해설 빈도부사 never는 일반동사 gave up 앞에 위치

7 ③
해설 '거의 ~ 않는'이라는 의미의 빈도부사는 seldom이나 hardly로, 일반동사 does 앞에 위치한다.

8 ④
해설 '종종'이라는 의미의 빈도부사는 often으로, be동사 is 뒤에 위치한다.

9 (1) They sometimes go to the movies.
(2) They are always in the house.

NOW REAL TEST 2 p. 084

1 Sally drives carelessly.

2 (1) high (2) late

3 ④
해설 ④는 형용사이고 나머지는 부사이다.

4 ②
해설 ① Amy can usually swim ~. ③ They are never late ~. ④ visit → visits ⑤ Sam seldom does ~.

5 (1) always plays (2) never plays

선생님, 헷갈려요! p. 086

1 (1) boring (2) surprised (3) tiring, tired

2 I watched a fantastic movie about baseball. The movie was very interesting. My friend Jesse watched a different movie. It was boring. Jesse was really disappointed by the movie.

Chapter 8
부가의문문, 비인칭주어, 4형식 문장

UNIT 15
부가의문문, 비인칭주어

PRACTICE p. 088

1 Billy has a twin brother, doesn't he?
2 Don't drink too much coffee, will you?
3 What season is it in Japan now?
4 It takes five minutes to the park by bike.

NOW REAL TEST 1 p. 089

1 It

2 That's → It's

3 (1) It takes two hours.
(2) It is 100 dollars.

4 (1) isn't it (2) don't they (3) shall we

5 ①
해설 ①은 '그것'이라는 의미의 지시대명사이고 나머지는 비인칭주어이다.

6 ②

7 (1) You aren't (= are not) hungry
(2) She likes shopping
(3) Let's go to the amusement park

8 ④
해설 주어진 문장의 it은 앞 문장의 a very special dress를 가리키는 지시대명사이다. ④는 지시대명사이고 나머지는 비인칭주어이다.

NOW REAL TEST 2 p. 091

1 Jinhi: Is it raining outside?
Minho: Yes, it is.

2 ④
해설 ① isn't he → doesn't he ② isn't Usain Bolt → isn't he ③ is he → isn't he ⑤ do you → will you

3 (1) You aren't interested in watching movies, are you?
(2) John had a lot of books, didn't he?

4 ④
해설 ④는 비인칭주어이고 나머지는 지시대명사이다.

5 This is rainy → It is rainy / there will be sunny → it will be sunny / will we? → shall we?

UNIT 16
4형식 문장

PRACTICE p. 093

1 I will buy you a new watch.
(또는 I will buy a new watch for you.)
2 Parents give their children love.
(또는 Parents give love to their children.)
3 My uncle made me a dress.
(또는 My uncle made a dress for me.)
4 Her smile brings me happiness.
(또는 Her smile brings happiness to me.)

NOW REAL TEST 1 p. 094

1 (1) They bought a good car for their parents.
(2) The teacher showed a painting to us.
(3) He gave the children some big help.
(4) I will buy some snacks for your friends.
(5) My sister cooked dinner for me.
(6) The doctor gave him some medicine.
(7) I will make a delicious cake for my son tomorrow.
(8) He sent a gift to her.
(9) Give others all of your clothes.
(10) My father made a nest for the birds.

2 buy a pair of shoes for him

3 (1) Jihyo a beautiful bag
(2) a nice car for Jihyo

4 ⑤
해설 동사가 ask이므로 to가 아니라 of가 되어야 한다.

5 • Today is my mom's birthday. I will give some flowers to her.
• My mom always cooks delicious food for me.

NOW REAL TEST 2 p. 096

1 to, for, of

2 (1) The man gave her a flower.
(2) The man gave a flower to her.

3 (1) The company bought him a new car.
(2) The company bought a new car for him.

4 ①, ③
해설 ① to → for ③ to → of

5 (1) a hat to (2) a cake for

6 ⓐ bought me a bag ⓑ made yummy cookies for me ⓒ gave me a doll

선생님, 헷갈려요! p. 098

1 ④
2 ②

Chapter 9
to부정사와 동명사

UNIT 17
to부정사

PRACTICE p. 100

1 I want to be a doctor.
2 Mr. Smith sang a song to please her.
3 To cook with children is fun. (또는 It is fun to cook with children.)
4 We lined up to buy some doughnuts.

NOW REAL TEST 1 p. 101

1 Her dream is to be a movie director.
(또는 Her dream is to become a movie director.)

2 to take

3 My mom wanted me to help her.

4 to tell the secret

5 (1) I turned on the fan to get some cool air.
(2) He reads a lot of books to get useful information from them.

6 take pictures to make my own album

7 (1) Steve's dream is to be a great scientist. (또는 Steve's dream is to become a great scientist.)
(2) I want to stay here.

8 (1) I don't want to watch TV all day long.
(2) I really hope to see her soon.

9 ⓐ to pass the exam
ⓑ not to be late for school

NOW REAL TEST 2 p. 103

1 (1) To solve math questions is very hard.
(2) It is easy for Jack to study English.

2 ⓐ go → to go (또는 going)
ⓒ Have → To have (또는 Having)

3 ①
해설 ② see → to see ③ To not sleep → Not to sleep ④ run → to run ⑤ get → to get

4 (1) 다시 만나서 무척 반갑습니다.
(2) 나는 새 자전거를 사기 위해 돈을 번다.
(3) 오래된 신문을 모으는 것은 쉽지 않다.
(4) Joyce는 자라서 작가가 되었다.
(5) 그런 일을 하는 것을 보니 너는 매우 이기적이다.
다른 것: (3)
해설 나머지는 to부정사의 부사적 용법이고, (3)은 주어의 역할을 하는 명사적 용법이다.

5 ④
해설 to부정사의 부정은 'not to+동사원형'이다.

UNIT 18
동명사

PRACTICE p. 105

1 My hobby is playing soccer in my free time.
2 Washing dirty cars is very hard.
3 They avoided entering the secret room.
4 Thank you for inviting me to this party.

NOW REAL TEST 1 p. 106

1 (가) sending (나) reading
2 We should finish doing our homework soon.
3 What about watching a movie this Saturday?
4 He is also good at play the violin. → He is also good at playing the violin. / Is he interested in sing, too? → Is he interested in singing, too?
5 Saving money to go to Canada was very hard to me.
6 finish washing
7 ②
해설 stop+-ing: ~하는 것을 멈추다
8 ④
해설 전치사의 목적어로 동사가 올 때는 동명사 형태로 써야 한다. (play → playing)

NOW REAL TEST 2 p. 108

1 (1) collecting (2) playing (3) reading
2 (1) Thank you for (your) inviting me to B1A4's concert.
(2) My favorite activity is taking pictures of animals.
3 ①
해설 mind와 enjoy는 동명사를 목적어로 취하는 동사이다.
4 ①, ④, ⑤
해설 ② to go ③ reading
5 (1) Taking naps is Eugene's faverite thing to do.
(2) Sam enjoys playing computer games and reading books.
(3) Harold enjoys playing soccer and reading books.
6 He is interested in watching the baseball game.
해설 전치사의 목적어로 동사가 올 때는 동명사 형태로 써야 한다.

선생님, 헷갈려요! p. 110

1 (1) to buy (2) to give
2 (1) to look up (2) seeing

memo

memo

memo

memo

memo